THE HASMONEAN REVOLT
REBELLION OR REVOLUTION

Steven L. Derfler

Ancient Near Eastern Texts and Studies
Volume 5
The Edwin Mellen Press
Lewiston/Lampeter/Queenston

Library of Congress Cataloging-in-Publication Data

Derfler, Steven Lee.
    The Hasmonean Revolt : rebellion or revolution / by Steven L.
Derfler.
       p.   cm. -- (Ancient Near Eastern Text and Studies ; vol. 5)
    Includes bibliographical references.
    ISBN   0-88946-258-5
    1. Jews--History--168 B.C.-135 A.D. 2. Maccabees. I. Title.
    II. Series: Ancient Near Eastern Text and Studies (Lewiston, N.Y.) ; v.5.
    DS121.7.D47   1990
    933'.04--dc20   89-12698
                                                CIP

> This is volume 5 in the continuing series
> Ancient Near Eastern Texts and Studies
> Volume 5 ISBN 0-88946-258-5
> ANETS Series ISBN 0-88946-085-X

A CIP catalog record for this book
is available from the British Library.

The Edwin Mellen Press   The Edwin Mellen Press
Box 450   Box 67
Lewiston, NY   Queenston, Ontario
USA 14092   CANADA L0S 1L0

The Edwin Mellen Press, Ltd.
Lampeter, Dyfed, Wales,
UNITED KINGDOM SA48 7DY

Printed in the United States of America

THE HASMONEAN REVOLT
REBELLION OR REVOLUTION

TABLE OF CONTENTS

LIST OF ABBREVIATIONS

AASOR	Annual of the American Schools of Oriental Research
ASOR	American Schools of Oriental Research
BA	Biblical Archaeologist
BASOR	Bulletin of the American schools of Oriental Research
BMC	British Museum Catalogue
BP I	Beth Pelet I
BS I	Beersheva I
B.Shearim	Beth Shearim I
CPJ	Corpus Papyrorum Judaicarum
Grace	American Excavations in the Athenian Agora IV
HarExSam	Harvard Excavations at Samaria 1908-10
IEJ	Israel Exploration Journal
JourJuristPap	Journal of Juristic Papyrology
Kypros	Kypros: Die Bibel und Homer
Meg I	Megiddo I
Olynthus	Excavations at Olynthus X
Ontario	Ancient Lamps in the Royal Ontario Museum I
PCC	Palestine Ceramic Chronology
Persian	The Material Culture of the Land of Israel in the Persian Era
QDAP	Quarterly of the Department of Antiquities of Palestine
Roeder	Aegyptische Bronzefiguren
Schloessinger	Ancient Lamps in the Schloessinger Collection, Qedem 8

SS III	Samaria-Sebaste III
TA	Tel Aviv Journal of Archaeology
TX	Tel Keisan
TN I	Tel en Nasbeh I
Tools	Tools and Weapons

LIST OF ILLUSTRATIONS

1. ALEXANDER THE GREAT. [L] Coin minted in Magnesia by Lysimachus. [R] Alabaster bust (Brooklyn Museum)

2. EXAMPLE OF A ZENON PAPYRUS. (Cairo Museum, #59003)

3. PTOLEMY II PHILADELPHUS. [L] Egyptianizing bust (Paris, Louvre). [R] Bronze bust from Herculaneum (Naples, Museo Nazionale)

4. ISOMETRIC VIEW OF THE TEMPLE AT IRAQ EL-AMIR, CAPITAL OF THE TOBIAD CLERUCHY.

5. PTOLEMY III EUERGETES. Coin Portrait.

6. PTOLEMY IV PHILOPATOR. Marble bust.

7. ANTIOCHUS III, THE GREAT. Marble bust (Paris, Louvre)

8. IMAGE OF THE TEMPLE IN JERUSALEM, by Franciscus Vitablus, 16th Century.

9. PLAN OF THE HELLENISTIC CITY OF JERUSALEM.

10. PTOLEMY V EPIPHANES. Coin Portrait.

11. ANTIOCHUS IV EPIPHANES. Coin Portrait.

12. MODEL OF THE HELLENISTIC CITY OF JERUSALEM.

I

BACKGROUND OF THE HASMONEAN REVOLT

The Hasmonean Revolt, the liberation movement that allowed for the rebirth of a Jewish State in Judea after four centuries of foreign domination, has been viewed in many different lights by scholars in various fields: history, economics, sociology and religion, to name a few. Each of these scholars, in his or her own way, puts forth many thought-provoking theories on the development of circumstances surrounding this revolt. However, in order to appreciate more fully this revolution and the nature of the emergent kingdom, a synthesis of all of these theories must be attempted in trying to understand the events that transpired.

In attempting to reconstruct the military, political, social, religious, and economic background that gave rise to this revolt, one needs to examine closely the nature of Judea prior to the actions of the 150's and 140's BCE. In other words, the seeds of the revolution appear to have been planted as a result of factors that began to develop as early as the first half of the Third and Second Centuries BCE--the period when the Levantine Coast was opened to the world of the west. With the advent of Alexander and his kingdom, the "oriental" nature of Syria/Palestine was forever to be altered. Centuries of close ties with the east would not be replaced by the "enlightened west." The shock of such

a change, although gradual, struck deep into the heart
of the Judean population, both Jewish and Gentile. Their
ability or inability to cope with this change would leave
a permanent impression on Judean life for centuries to
come. Therefore, the examination of this initial century
and a half is essential in understanding the nature of
the state. One needs to examine the social conditions
and composition of Judea in this 250 years and its
relation to Hellenization. Closely knit into the fabric
is the religious tenor of the community. What was the
official and unofficial response to this foreign
incursion? Domestic politics and political institutions
appear to be next on the agenda with regard to fields to
explore: what was the legal, or paralegal, framework
that the social conditions rise from and react to?
Finally, a breakdown of the Alexandrian empire leading
to the creation of rival mini-kingdoms, such as those of
the Seleucids and Ptolemies, brought about additional
problems for the various local communities. Seleucid
domination and subsequent Antiochan persecutions of the
160's BCE appear to be the final "straws" that forced a
coalition comprised of nearly every segment of Judean
society to rise up and forcibly expel the foreign
oppressive powers that had for too long dominated the
district of Judea.

Granted, there have been several studies
undertaken, but each appears to be accentuating a
particular discipline, Although each field is an entity
to itself, the examination of any subject needs to
integrate more fully all areas of research. There indeed
may be overlap in some cases, but this would only serve
to strengthen the threads that are needed to weave

together the fabric of this nature. With this background explored in depth, one can more fully appreciate the world that John Hyrcanus I entered into in 135/4 BCE; and perhaps get a greater sense of the man and his actions based on events surrounding the birth of the kingdom he so suddenly inherited after the murder of his father and brothers at 'Ain Duq.

II

SOCIAL CONDITIONS

The Zenon Papyri

If it were not for a group of documents known as the
Zenon Papyri, our information about the social conditions
and demographic make-up of Judea would be nearly
nonexistent. (See Appendix One.) They supply a plethora
of primary data, factual material, that leaves little to
the imagination.[1] This data basically deals with contact
between the foreign element and native population of
Judea during Ptolemaic rule, especially during the years
of 260-258 BCE. These documents give one a reading of
the process of fusion of Eastern and Western

---

[1] For all references in Hebrew Bible, Holy
Scriptures According to Masoretic Text. JPS, 1955.

For all references in the Septuagint, The
Septuagint Version of the Old Testament, Zondervan, 1972.

For further information on the Zenon Papyri, see
V. Tcherikover, "Palestine in Light of the Zenon Papyri,"
Tarbiz 4 (1933) , pp. 226-247, 354-365; Tarbiz 5 (1934)
pp. 37-44.

civilizations culturally, economically and to an extent,
religiously. In 259 BCE, Apollonius, then the Egyptian
Minister of Finance, sent out a large delegation on what
today would be termed a "fact-finding mission." (See
Appendix Two, Map 2.) This group broke down into smaller
units and went their separate ways throughout Palestine.
The papyri enable one to trace their journeys in the
land. These groups went, for example, to Gaza, Adoraim,
and Marissa in one segment; Strato's Tower via
Jerusalem,, Jericho, Acco, and Bethlehem in another; even
to such far and distant lands as Hauran and Nabatea in
others.[2] Bear in mind that "smaller group" in this sense
still meant an entirely self-sufficient "portable city"
with a total service staff that was hired from local
populations as well as brought from Egypt.   It even
appears that the group actively sought close contact as
they traveled through the land, even to the extent of
obtaining wives.   In the Vienna Papyrus (PER.Inv.N 2
24.552 gr) one finds a statement by Ptolemy II
Philadelphus (285-246 BCE) that speaks of "soldiers and
other settlers in Syria and Phoenicia who took wives from
among native girls."[3] Therefore, if the king mentioned
and appeared to condone it, the practise must surely have
been a widespread one. Orders indicate that these were
not slaves but wives, indicating an official sanction to

---

[2]F.M. Able, "la liste geographique du papyrus 71 de
Zenon," RB 32, (1923) pp. 406ff. See Appendix 2, Map of
Travels in Zenon Papyri.

[3]H. Liebesny, "Ein Erlass des Koenigs Ptolemaios II
Philadelphos uber die Beklaration von Vieh und Skhurn in
Syrien und Phownikien,"Aegyptus 16 (1936) pp. 257ff.

the rite of intermarriage.[4]

A prime example of this interaction between populations can be witnessed in Corpus Papyrorum Judaicarum (hereafter CPJ #1). (See Appendix One, #1.) Several ethnic elements appear to be involved in the sale of a slave girl who was with her owner, originally from Cnidus, now one of Tobiah's men in Palestine. Zenon, acting on behalf of Apollonius, is the buyer. Participants as indicated were a Greek, a Macedonian, and two Persians who were Greek and Jewish respectively in origin. This example reveals what a "melting pot" the army truly was at the time.[5]

In spite of intercourse of this nature, one basic problem still existed: the Greeks (and their Hellenized Egyptian comrades) considered the local population to be inferior. Earlier, Alexander the Great saw the necessity of wooing the local population and its rulers. thus gaining support for his empire regionally.[6] However, after Alexander's death, the honeymoon was over and political and economic reality set in. The Ptolemaic Dynasty that succeeded Alexander in Egypt knew full well the difference between the victors and the vanquished. The only exceptions to this were the

---

[4] Ibid., p. 258.

[5] V. Tcherikover in A. Schalit, The Hellenistic Age: World History of the Jewish People, (1972), p.90.

[6] V. Tcherikover, Hellenistic Civilization and the Jews, (1954), p.7.

1. ALEXANDER THE GREAT. (L) Coin Minted In Magnesia. (R) Alabaster Bust [Brooklyn Museum]

few local princes or leaders who the Ptolemies felt were essential for internal stability and continued consolidation of power. It also was beneficial that these local leaders desired to be Hellenized as well, inferring a **pro forma** acceptance into the greater Hellenistic World. This action in no way implied that the native Judean culture was inferior to that of the Greek world; rather, it was merely a practical political consideration of a sycophantic nature coupled with the desire to become a greater part of this foreign world.

2. AN EXAMPLE OF A ZENON PAPYRUS. (Cairo Museum #59003)

In light of this arrogant attitude on behalf of the Greeks and Ptolemies, it was no wonder that a popular conception was that the Eastern, or Oriental, being was a slave to the Western, or Hellenistic, person. As a result of this, the disparity in cultural eloquence **vis--a-vis** life-style and education between Palestine and Egypt, with relation to Greece, only widened the rift. A direct outgrouth was a rise in slave trafficking.[7] In spite of its "illegality" on a private or individual basis, it still thrived as an underworld activity. One particular fragment, PCZ 59093, dealt with exportation of slaves and benefits caused by it.[8] (See Appendix One, # 59093). Still another, PSI 406, related similar activities by other lesser officials.[9]

The situation as applied to land, land ownership, and labor conditions is also revealed by the papyri, but to a lesser extent. The balm that Alexander wished to apply in attempting an alleviation of the difference between the conquered and conqueror was abruptly removed after his death. This balm was in the form of allowing local Persian and Judean princes to retain some control of the land after the Macedonian

---

[7]   For more on slavery in Ptolemaic Egypt, see W.C. Westerman, Upon Slavery in Ptolemaic Egypt, 1929.

[8]   V. Tcherikover, "Palestine Under the Ptolemies", Mitzraim 4-5 (1937), p. 88. See Appendix One, Zenon Papyri, PCZ 59093.

[9]   PSI 406, Publicazioni della Societa Italiana per la Ricerca dei Papiri Greci e Latini in Egitto, Papiri Greci e Latini, Firenze.

takeover.[10] Yet in 323 BCE, when the Diodochi began to
divide the Empire, this policy was reversed, with such
kings as Ptolemy I proclaiming total "ownership" and
authority over the land. In essence, he proclaimed that
all the land belonged to Egypt, with very little private
ownership.[11] However, it is assumed that this nearly
total control was clouded by the magnanimous gesture of
allowing a very few local princes to have some autonomy
so as to keep the local population in hand. Needless to
say, this land was not in great amount. Most of the land
anyway, the most fertile, was of the former Persian king
and his family. It was confiscated by the Ptolemies at
the outset.[12]

     A site in lower Galil, Beth-Anath, most likely
gives one a good indication of the social conditions of
the peasant class at this time. (See Appendix Two, Map
2.) This estate, owned by Apollonius, is described in
PSI 554.[13] This document describes an argument over a
wheat transaction between Apollonius' manager, Melas, and
the deliverers of the wheat. In the argument, both sides
cite official documents to enhance their respective
cases. Unfortunately, the papyrus is damaged, so the

---

[10] E. Bickerman, From Ezra to the Last of the
Maccabees, (1962), pp. 41-50.

[11] M. Hengel, Hellenism and Judaism, (1974), pp.
18ff.

[12] V. Tcherikover, op. cit., (1954), p. 54, f.n. 87.

[13] V. Tcherikover in A. Schalit, p. 94, f.n. 14,15.
PSI 554, see f.n. 9.

outcome of the dispute will probably be forever unknown
to us. Further along in the same document, another
dispute is witnessed over the quality of raisins and
their subsequent confiscation. In essence, one finds a
test of the rights and privileges of a designated tax-
farmer, the **"komomisthotes"**, who acted on behalf of the
kings, and the rights and privileges of the local
population that, both in spirit and letter of the law,
he controlled.

Based on the papyrus, it appears that a couple
of conclusions can be reached concerning peasant life in
Palestine. First, these members of the local populations
lived on what could be termed the "royal land", and they
were allowed to till this land under certain conditions.
Second, these conditions required payment of a portion
of their production as a tax and rent, set at a certain
level by contract.[14]

What of the rich peasantry, those owning land
and/or enjoying a few privileges? They are rather
accurately described in CPJ #6. (See Appendix One, #6).
The main character in this document is Jaddua, a Jewish
farmer living within a greater Jewish population. Two
letters included discuss an "upstart" Jewish farmer, a
powerful man, who had no fear of any government officials
on the local or even regional level, nor any fear of
acting in a manner that was obviously contrary to those
officials' wishes. In addition, the text reveals a
unified support of the villagers against foreign
authority. Apparently two classes of peasantry did unite

---

[14] This system is a direct descendent of that used
by the Ptolemies in Egypt. See W. Tarn, Hellenistic
Civilization, (1952), pp. 197-203.

to form a common front with regard to economic policy. As the government became more deeply embroiled in this controversy, so more deeply did they seek non-violent means to solving the situation. In other words, the rich peasants, at times more often than not, had their own way locally.[15]

Another indication of the social situation in Palestine concerns Jews living amongst the rest of the general population, and not only in Judea. In the Zenon Papyri again one finds the names of Jews who were in contact with Apollonius' caravans.[16] Apparently the Tobiads were considered a wealthy family of local chieftains who played a major role within the sphere of the Hellenization process of the Jewish population. Some scholars, such as Mazar, believed their ancestry to be rooted in the Israelite Period, and coming from a priestly lineage.[17]

During the rule of Ptolemy II Philadelphus, it is documented that the family headed a military "cleruchy" in Transjordan. These men even appeared to assist the travelling bands of Apollonius when they were in Transjordan. They were referred to as "Tobiah's men"

---

[15] Appendix One, Zenon Papyri, CPJ 6.

[16] For references to the Tobiads in the Zenon Papyri, see Appendix One, CPJ 2a, 2b, 2c, 2d, 4, 5.

[17] B. Mazar,"The House of Tobiah", Tarbiz 12, (1941), p. 122 and "Ben Tabal and Beth Tuviya", EI 4 (1956), p. 249 ff. It appears that Tobiah himself was related to the High Priest Eliashiv, who arranged for Tobiah to have a "Chamber" in the Temple, cf. Neh. 13:4f.

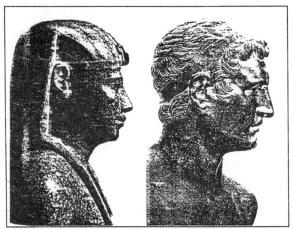

3. PTOLEMY II PHILADELPHUS. (L) Egyptianizing statue [Paris, Louvre] (R) Bronze bust from Herculaneum [Naples, Museo Nazionale]

or "Tobiah's cavalry".[18] Another document mentions the fact that even a portion of the Transjordan was called the "Land of Tobiah".[19] In truth, however, the Tobiad's were not Ammonite by nature, as the location of their landholdings would suggest; rather, they were native Jerusalemites who became referred to as Ammonites due to the geographical location.

Of what importance was this man Tobiah to the Egyptian rulers? Based on the Zenon Papyri, it appears that a fairly intimate and important relationship was maintained by Ptolemy II with Tobiah. Granted, it was a fairly usual practise for one to offer gifts to the king as a matter of etiquette. However, one letter discussed the gift to Apollonius of a set of rare animals

---

[18] A cleruchy is an area of land given as military allotment by the king. The people were military settlers placed by the king in order to secure the land and promise continued military presence.

[19] Appendix One, Zenon Papyri, CPJ 2d:6.

destined for the Alexandrian Zoo.[20] In yet another,
Apollonius receives "gifts" of four slaves and a
eunuch.[21] These very costly gifts show not only an
important and close relationship with the royal family
in Alexandria, but also a very independent position
politically. This closeness is further shown by the king
via his personal confidence in Tobiah.   Tobiah is
appointed head of the cleruchy in Transjordan (infra.p.
21) and given the task of defending the borders. This
in itself is fairly astonishing to have a Jewish prince
in enough confidence to defend Egypt's interests.

However, Tobiah's family most likely was not
the typical Jewish family by any stretch of the
imagination. The high degree of Hellenization within the
family is very evident in many of Tobiah's letters.
Tobiah obviously used a Greek secretary to write all of
his correspondance. This secretary made use of all the
standard Greek formulae, including ones such as **"polle
charis tois theois"**, "many thanks to the gods", a sure
sign of acceptance of the Hellenized way.[22] It appears
that Jewish aristocracy was striving to remold the Jewish
way of life yet not necessarily change the religion. The
matter was not religious, rather political and cultural.
However, as will be seen, politics and religion ofttimes
come hand in hand and these aristocratic attempts in fact
spilled over and preserved certain ideals that were not

---

[20] Appendix One, Zenon Papyri, <u>CPJ</u> 4.

[21] Apendix One, Zenon Papyri, <u>CPJ</u> 5.

[22] M. Hengel, <u>op. cit.</u>, (1974), pp. 59 and 267 ff;
and <u>CPJ</u> 1, Appendix One.

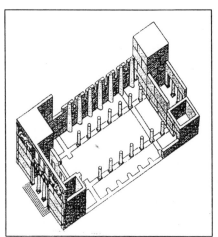

4. AN ISOMETRIC VIEW OF THE TEMPLE AT IRAQ EL-AMIR, CAPITAL OF THE TOBIAD CLERUCHY.

truly compatible with traditional Judaism.

Power and the Role of Taxation

As one continues to trace this family in the next generation, one sees an even more astonishing role being played by Joseph, son of Tobiah. However, caution is necessary when reviewing the stories of Joseph as detailed by the historian Josephus.[23] Care must be taken since Josephus is indeed a literary source, and he has often been doubted, or at least questioned, in other historical incidents.[24] Power can be interpreted as being primarily financial, acting on behalf of Ptolemy III Euergetes (246-221 BCE) in the field of tax reform in the provinces.[25] Prior to the deeds enacted by Joseph, tax collecting was done by local individuals who obtained permission from the king to become "tax-farmers" of the city.[26] This entire practice stemmed from Egyptian prototypes.[27] Joseph proposed to centralize tax collection under one person, himself, by promising the king that he would double annually the wheat that

---

[23] Josephus _AJ_ XII, pp. 160-200.

previously had been collected.[23] In other words, the
8,000 talents of wheat mentioned as being collected in
the past year would be doubled to 16,000.[24] However,
care must be taken as this figure, quoted by Josephus,
is apparently exaggerated.[25]

It seems evident that Joseph's system
infiltrated every stratum of society via the use of
spies, in order to achieve his goals of tax collection.[26]
The Book of Koheleth, written in the decade prior to the
Hasmonean Revolt, reflects the feeling of fear that was
a constant burden on the people.[27] This atmosphere
indicates that not all of Joseph's power was in the
financial arena. It seemed that many Greek cities
refused to accept the reform of Ptolemy II, and in a way,
revolted against Joseph's authority. This was expected
by Egypt, so soldiers were given to Joseph to use as he
saw fit to crush potential revolts in such towns as

---

[23] M. Hengel, op. cit., p.27.

[24] Josephus, AJ XIII, 175f.

[25] Heironymous, In Daniel 11:5, states that in fact
all of the income that Ptolemy II received **from Egypt in
entirety** amounted to only 14,000 talents. See also
Diodorus XIX,56,5.

[26] S. Zeitlin, op. cit., v.1, p. 57.

[27] Also called Ecclesiasticus by Ben Sirach, 10:20,
LVX, p. 82.

Ashkelon and Scythopolis.[28]

Following 221 BCE, under the rule of Ptolemy IV Philopater, the Egyptian throne became weak, rife with internal troubles.[29] As a result, now more than ever, an equally powerful Egyptian presence was needed in Palestine to offset pressure from Antiochus III of Syria. Joseph, son of Tobiah, was seen as the key to a strong Egyptian policy and he became one of the powers to contend with on behalf of Egypt. The essential element to

6 . P T O L E M Y I V PHILOPATOR.Marble bust.

remember, though, is that, although Joseph was Jewish, his rise to power was not necessarily to benefit the Jewish community of Palestine. Those who did benefit most likely did so as a result of their own initiative and Hellenistic outlook on life; rather than more traditional values. On the contrary, Joseph's power as

---

[28] M. Hengel, op. cit., p. 27f.

[29] W. Tarn, op. cit., (1952), p. 21f. "Ptolemy III had allowed his army to decay, and his son Ptolemy IV was an art-loving voluptuary, who left his government to his strong and unscrupulous minister Sosibus." See also M. Hengel, op. cit., (1974), pp. 8-10.

the new tax-collector caused increased animosity among his populace, as well as fostered hatred due to the conception that he indeed had turned his back on his brethren. In addition, jealousy and envy was yet even greater in the Greek cities of Palestine, and , as was the case in Ashkelon and Scythopolis earlier, harsh measures were enacted in order to accomplish the will of Ptolemy IV.

Joseph truly had become more imbued with Greek ideals and values than Jewish ones. He aligned himself more with the Greek perception that any means would in fact be justified by the end result. Alexandria, the jewel of Egypt, was regarded as the focal point of all life, rather than Jerusalem. All of the modest traditions of Jerusalem and Judean Jewry were a thing of the past for him, and Joseph saw himself as being extremely worldly in all affairs. Josephus the historian even states that Joseph was the first to open his house in Jerusalem to the Hellenistic world and all of its glory.[30]

The third generation of Tobiads, that of Hyrcanus and his brother, reveals how rivalry amongst brothers can be turned, exploited by greater outside powers. Again, one must caution against the use of Josephus as a primary source, as many of the stories are pure legend found in family chronicles.[31] The principal relevant episode concerns a trip taken to Alexandria in the years 210-209 BCE on behalf of his old and infirm

---

[30]   Josephus, AJ, XII, pp. 187ff.

[31]   See note 24 above.

father, Joseph.[37]   As legend has it, Hyrcanus,
supposedly the favorite son of Joseph, was sent to Egypt
to congratulate Ptolemy IV on the birth of a son.   He
went because he was allegedly the best schooled in the
Greek style.   The wealth of presents from the Tobiad
family is difficult to believe, said to be one-third of
Joseph's worth.   But what were Hyrcanus' real motives?
Apparently he was **not** the next in line for his father's
job of head tax-collector, and he dearly coveted it.
Therefore, according to Josephus, his true motive was in
securing a favorable letter from Ptolemy IV to show to
his family.

      Meanwhile, the other brothers, learning of
this, wrote to their friends in Alexandria, setting out
a contract that called for the death of their brother,
Hyrcanus.[38] Joseph himself was infirm and unable to act,
so the question of succession became a hotly contested
issue.   Ptolemy IV wrote a very favorable letter on
behalf of Hyrcanus, infuriating the brothers even more.
In addition, Joseph was extremely angry with his son, yet
did nothing because of his fear of the king.[39]

      Following Joseph's death, a majority of the
people, including the High Priest, sided with the older

---

[37]   Josephus AJ XII, 196-218.

[38]   Ibid., 218.

[39]   Ibid., 220f.

7. ANTIOCHUS III, THE GREAT.
Marble bust [Paris, Louvre]

brothers.[40]   However, Hyrcanus was able to buy his way into the position and placed himself as the official representative of the king, supported by the pro-Ptolemaic faction in Judea. At this point, the brothers decided to enlist actively the aid of the opposition, Syria, under the rule of Antiochus III(223-187 BCE). In fact, it is well documented that Simeon the High Priest even welcomed Antiochus III to Jerusalem.[41]

These acts forced Hyrcanus from Judea altogether, and he fled to the family's ancestral home in Transjordan, to live out his days fighting the Nabateans.[42] Upon the ascent of

---

[40]   When Hyrcanus came to Jerusalem, all of the gates to the city were shut to him, apparently on order of the High Priest, Simon the Just.

[41]   Josephus _AJ_ XII, 229.

[42]   _Ibid._, 234. Josephus calls them "Arabs", but it can be a given that they were Nabateans.   See J. Lawlor,_The Nabateans in Historical Perspective_, Baker, 1974.

Antiochus IV Epiphanes in Syria (175-164 BCE),[43] Hyrcanus found himself in what he saw as an untenable position and committed suicide.[44] The policies instituted by Antiochus IV were designed to strengthen and unify the Seleucid Kingdom. Hyrcanus did not act in the usual manner either as a landowner or tax-farmer. Rather, his attitude apparently was one of a small, independent prince, as described by Josephus.[45] Antiochus IV could not, and would not tolerate this kind of activity. Therefore, the only option for Hyrcanus other than war seemed to be suicide.

In light of all his activities, Hyrcanus was seen as a figure who acted strangely during these last few years. However, this again is only true if he is viewed as a Jew and is cast in the role of a traditional Jew within the framework of Jerusalemite Judaism. If Hyrcanus is cast as a Hellenizer, then the situation would not seem quite so odd. The question raised is, would a Hellenizer be caught in a position of untenable opposition to a Seleucid king? Hyrcanus broke from the old ways and his father's traditionalism in order to view

---

[43] Seleucus III Soter ruled Syria from 187-175 BCE.

[44] Josephus places this occurrence after seven years; yet again we find error in his chronology, as it should be twenty-five years.

[45] Josephus _AJ_ XII, 236ff. Perhaps the period of 'independence' is seven years as stated in footnote 38. After M. Hengel, _op. cit._, (1974) p. 274f.

the larger Greek world and be an active part of it.[46]
However, viewing the greater Greek world did in no way
pressure blind loyalty to any Hellenistic state. Bear
in mind that a number of philosophical differences
existed between all of the Hellenistic states, Seleucid
and Ptolemaic included. With the strong rivalry that was
evident between these two in particular, there is no
reason to assume that an untenable position with one
might not be tacitly supported by the other. It is held
by some that Hyrcanus, in a way, even succeeded in
establishing a form of Jewish Kingdom; small, yet to an
extent, workable. It failed because he aspired to too
much politically with his limited resources. This was
his downfall, a too weak base against the power of
Syria.[47]

---

[46]   See M. Hengel, _ibid._,pp 103-107.

[47]   _Ibid._, p. 275-277.

The Role of the Clergy

The social order in Jerusalem at this time was called a "theocracy" by Josephus.[48] However, today modern scholarship would rather use the term "hierocracy", or "priestly rule". The High Priest supposedly represented the Judean population in every way, both spiritually and politically, and the literature of the time reflects this. One such author, Hecataeus of Abdera, stated that there were 1,500 priests functioning.[49] His statements most likely were referring to only those priests found in and around Jerusalem. (infra.p. 35) In his eyes, the role of High Priest may have been that of an intermediary, perhaps parallelling a concept utilized by Egyptian priests at that time.[50] The origin of these priests, as pointed out by Hecataeus, came during the life of Moses, when Moses chose the best men and put them as heads of the people, priests and judges,   Diodorus   relates   this   passage   from Hecataeus'statement:

> Therefore, the Jews never
> had a king and the function

---

[48]   Josephus, Contra Apion II, 165.

[49]   H. Lewy, "Hekataios von Abdera", ZNW 31 (1932), pp. 117ff.

[50]   For more on ancient Egyptian religion and the role of priests, see H. Frankfort, Egyptian Religion, 1972.

> of representation
> (prostasia) was given to
> the priest, who excelled
> all others in wisdom and
> superior qualities. They
> call him the High Priest
> and consider him a Divine
> Messenger who brings them
> God's commandments. He is
> said to transmit God's
> commandments at assemblies
> of the people and other
> meetings, and the Jews show
> such great obedience to
> these things that they
> immediately prostrate
> themselves before the High
> Priest who interprets to
> them God's words. [51]

Apparently, the priestly class was the only group closely examined, indicating them to be perhaps the only ones that could attract any strangers to the cult.

Another strong indicator of the power and prestige of the High Priest in Jerusalem's society is reflected in the Letter of Aristeas. It was written by an Alexandrian Jew under the guise of a person named Aristeas, a Greek within the court of Ptolemy II Philadelphus.[52] The narrative includes brief descriptions of the journey from Alexandria to Jerusalem,

---

[51]   Diodorus XL, pp. 5-6.

[52]   M. Hadas, Aristeas to Philocrates, 1951.

as well as a description of the city of Jerusalem.
However, the main narrative deals with the High Priest
Eleazar and the Temple service.   It is of great
importance, as it is the work of a Jewish author in the
Diaspora writing about the Jerusalem priestly society.[53]
As a stranger, it is no wonder that Aristeas was dazzled
and impressed by the Temple service.   However, even to
Jerusalemite Jewry, there was not only a profound
admiration but a feeling of awe.

       Another author, Jesus ben Sirach, also is able
to convey the feelings aroused by the priestly class and
the great mystical power that they held over the
populace.[54] He described wonderfully the appearance of
Simon the Just, well illustrating how the external
splendor surrounding the High Priest could make a lasting

---

[53] Letter of Aristeas, pp. 83-181.

[54] R.H. Charles, Apocrypha and Pseudepigrapha of
the Old Testament, (1913), I, 168-517.

impression on all who visited the Temple.[55]

For the priests themselves, the Temple was not only the centre of worship, but a base for political and financial power. The Temple was the repository for gold and silver from Jews from all over the world, as well as public and private funds of Judeans.[56] The political power of the priests was viewed as stemming from

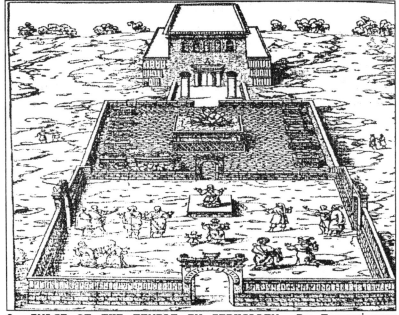

8. IMAGE OF THE TEMPLE IN JERUSALEM. By Franciscus Vitablus, 16th Century.

---

[55]   Ben Sirach 50:1-24, LXX, pp. 119-120.

[56]   II Macc. 3:10ff.   Second Book of Maccabees, S. Zeitlin, ed., (1954), pp. 119-120.

"ancestral law" and had full governmental approval. This
governmental approval even appears to grant special
protection from the Seleucid king to the Temple precinct.
Josephus describes a number of documents that refer to
this protection. For example, one such document written
during the reign of Antiochus III forbade strangers (non-
Jews) from entering the Temple.[57] Other documents
preserved by Josephus tell of edicts forbidding the
approach of unclean animals to the inner city of
Jerusalem and breeding them near to the Temple Mount.
All of this special protection was due not to Syrian
interest in the cult, but rather to gain support and
ensure stable, direct control over the Temple by the
priests and ultimately, by the Seleucids. The Seleucids
were said at times to have even contributed to the Temple
treasury.

---

[57] Josephus, AJ XII, 145. See also E. Bickerman,
"Une proclamation Seleucide relative au temple de
Jerusalem", Syria 25 (1946-48), pp. 67ff.

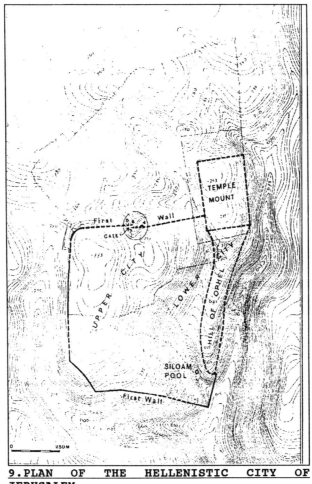

9. PLAN OF THE HELLENISTIC CITY OF JERUSALEM.

Yet within this priestly class a social division was also evident, and slowly a breakdown within the class could be seen; a direct result of Hellenism. Since the return from the Exile, the priestly class had been divided into families.[58] A majority of the families seemed to have lived outside the city and only came in when their priestly rotation duties were required.[59] Therefore, their way of life was more rural than urban.

Priestly bonds not withstanding, a great economic and social disparity was created between the rich, urbanized Jerusalemite priestly class and the poorer, rural priestly families. With this fact in mind, it is not surprising to learn that the strong push for Hellenization came from the rich Jerusalemite priests; and the protagonists of the the Hasmoneans, the Maccabean priests, came from the small, remote village of Modi'in.

The main difficulty in examining the priestly class and its families lies in the fact that only one family, the Onidas, are historically documented.[60] Other names of priests and families are recorded, but very little is known about them. These are found mainly in lists of priests returning from the Babylonian Exile.[61] Still

---

[58]   Nehemiah 11:10-15.

[59]   For archaeological evidence of this rotation, see Y. Aharoni, "The Israelite Sanctuary at Arad", NDBA, (1971), p. 36.

[60]   Josephus, AJ XI, XII.

[61]   Ezra 2 and Nehemiah 7, for example.

others are mentioned in inscriptions, such as the priestly
family of Hezir, buried on the Mount of Olives.[62]

The Secular Aristocracy

The same difficulty holds true for the secular
aristocracy. Again, only one family is well documented,
that of the Tobiads (supra.p. 17ff). Long registers of
names are recorded, but once more, those are only names.[63]
Nehemiah speaks of " nobles and elders". It seems likely
that if they existed in the 5th Century BCE with Nehemiah,
they then probably survive down through the Hellenistic
age. A **"gerousia"**, or "council of elders", was in
operation, yielding evidence that an aristocratic class
appeared to have a major influence, or even direct rule,
over the populace. This seems to be patterned directly
after institutions found in Greece at the time.[64] Main
revenues of this council came from agricultural taxes.
This nobility also tried in many ways to amass land for
themselves. However, Nehemiah fought for peasant rights
and strived to end the economic slavery that entrapped the
common people.[65] His attempts at reform succeeded, as is

---

[62] S. Klein, Ancient Monuments in the Kidron Valley
(1954), p. 59f.

[63] Ezra and Nehemiah, op. cit.

[64] For a more comprehensive look at the "gerousia",
see V. Tcherikover, "Was Jerusalem a Polis?' IEJ 5.4
(1964), pp. 61-78.

[65] Nehemiah 5:1.

related by Hecateus, via Diodorus. It is stated that a special law was enacted in order to keep small landholders from selling out their property.[66] Apparently this law survived into the Hellenistic 00period,allowing for compromise and a relatively peaceful co-existence between peasants and nobles. This bond is evident in the broad support for the eventual Hasmonean Revolt.

As the Hellenistic power became firmly entrenched in Judea, so too did its customs and ideas. The Hellenization process brought on by the Tobiads, and especially Joseph ben Tobiah (supra.p.20f), according to Josephus, "had brought the Jewish people from poverty and a state of weakness to some splendid opportunities of life."[67]

The Creation of a Middle Class

The most easily influenced people came from the rising class of wealthy bourgeoisie; government officials, agents, tax-collectors, and merchants. For the first time their power could be felt, used, and at times, manipulated. the bureaucratic class that became successful in Jerusalem, epitomized by the Tobiads, obtained their riches via tax collecting and tax farming, not trade.[68] It is no small wonder that a class hatred

---

[66] Diodorus, XL,7.

[67] Josephus, AJ, XII, 171ff.

[68] It should be noted, however, that the rich merchant class was not a major part of this group within Jerusalem's society. Wealth via trade came through

began to form in the first part of Seleucid control of
Palestine, 200-180 BCE. Ben Sirach traces the rising of
strife eloquently, seen as a result of the Hellenization
process that was enjoying enormous success now, implying
that the rich take advantage of the poor and greet the
poor with malice. Within the power structure, there is
literally no hope for the poor to go up against the rich.
One must bide one's time and be faithful to the law and
authority. The only way to triumph in the long run is
through study of (learning) knowledge, wisdom, and
morality. The implication, therefore, is that the rich
are akin to wickedness, and the poor are the strict
adherents of humility and morality.[69]

The Lower Stratum

The lower classes make up the final segment of
Jerusalem's social stratigraphy in both rural and urban
settings. However, direct evidence is virtually nonexistent. Small peasant landowners constituted a majority

---

overseas economy, and the group in control was the Greek
population in the coastal cities such as Gaza and
Ashkelon. V. Tcherikover, Hellenistic Civilization and
the Jews, (1954), pp. 91-117. Some examples attesting
to this in antiquity are: Letter of Aristeas 114-
speaking of spice trade controlled by Nabateans, not
Jews; Neh. 13:16 discusses the food commodity trade in
the hands of the Tyrians.

[69] V. Tcherikover, ibid., pp. 145-148; amd G.W.E.
Nicklesburg, Jewish Literature Between the Bible and
Mishnah, (1981), pp. 55-70.

(of the population) whose land was protected by laws
enacted against the "voracious appetite" of the wealthy
landholders (supra.p.38f). Yet no one discusses the size
of these landholdings, means of cultivation, or how they
fit into the economy. The peasant craftsmen of these
lower classes, the "urban proletariat", are merely
mentioned.[70] Their rise in economic status was a direct
result of the rise of the upper class and its desire for
luxury items. The Hellenization of the upper classes
undoubtedly benefited the lower classes who supplied those
whims and desires and needs; yet, at the same time,
resentment grew. This resentment developed not only in
the class conflict between rich and poor, but in
traditionalism versus Hellenism (religiously and
culturally). Finally, a political triangle emerged
pitting nationalists against pro-Seleucids against pro-
Ptolemies. The gaps could not be bridged and, along with
the political and religious persecution in the 160's,
caused Judea to rapidly head towards civil war.

---

70 Ben Sirach 38, LXX, pp. 105-108; Nehemiah 3.

III

THE POLITICAL SITUATION

The political situation in Palestine in the 3rd and 2nd Centuries BCE shifted from Ptolemaic Rule (302-198 BCE) to Seleucid Rule (198-164 BCE). (See Appendix Two, Map 3). In spite of the differences seen in Syrian and Egyptian rule, one major fact remains: both of these Hellenistic states were direct continuations of the much more ancient eastern kingdoms that existed prior to Greek control by Alexander the Great and his successors. Habits and ways of life ingrained for hundreds, if not thousands of years, are hard pressed to be thrown out or even substantially moderated; and Syria and Egypt were no exceptions. Even though rulers and ruling populations may change, the land and local population remain a constant. Ways of life that have been proven will most likely continue regardless of outside pressures.[71]

The Hasmonean and the Hellenistic State

The sole major difference between the Hasmonean State (infra.p.89) and the other Hellenistic states rested in the source of power. Both the Seleucid and

---

[71] For further light on this idea, see E.R. Goodenough, "The Political Philosophy of the Hellenistic Kingship", Yale Classical Studies, I, (1928), pp. 55f; and Rafal Taubenschlag, The Law of Greco-Roman Egypt in Light of the Papyri, (1972).

Ptolemaic kingdoms derived their power from dynasties established by force via adventurous leaders. The king was seen as a god, and although less true for the Seleucids than the Ptolemies, as in ancient Egypt, was entitled to all of the attributes and privileges of the ancient pharoah. He was the only source of law and justice in the land. As a result, he could do no wrong. All of the vestments of an absolute ruler were conferred upon him by the priests. He was the direct link betwen God and man, and everything needed his approval. This concept did not necessarily compromise the people's view of the king as god. All of the lands of Egypt were, in theory, his; as were all of the lands that were conquered by his sword. This too became his private property to do with as he saw fit. The title of a "totalitarian regime" is appropriate here.[72]

In Syria, the same kind of apparel seems to have prevailed with regard to the king. Here, the kingdom was, in essence, a direct continuation of the earlier Persian kingdom. The land was seen as **"Doriktetos ge"**, or the "land conquered by the spear"; the victor being the sole master, with all of the concepts pertaining to the spoils of war applied.[73]

---

[72] For more on the Ptolemaic Kingdom, see E. Bevan, History of Egypt under the Ptolemaic Dynasty,1927; C.B.Wells, "Ptolemaic Administration in Egypt", Journ. Jurist. Pap. III,(1941); W.W. Tarn, Hellenistic Civilization, (1952),pp.126-176; E.E. Rice, The Grand Procession of Ptolemy Philadelphus, (1983).

[73] For more on the Seleucid Kingdom, see E. Bevan, The House of Seleucus, 1902; E. Bickerman, Institutions de Seleucids, 1938; P.K.Hitti, History of Syria, 1951, ch. 6; W. Tarn, Hellenistic Civilization, 1952, pp. 126-176; M.M.Austen, The Hellenistic World from Alexander to the Roman Conquest,1981.

Bear in mind that the theory does not always mirror reality, and neither the Seleucids nor the Ptolemies were totally successful in running their respective Hellenistic states as planned. Both on political and economic planes, theory and practise did not correspond. Politically, all power was to reside with the king, as he was considered to be the law. If the regent was weak or young, as was the case with Ptolemy V, power would need to be vested in advisors. As a result, a group of advisors or ministers in actuality would run the states whether from Alexandria, or from the city of Seleuceia, followed by its successor as capital, Antioch. The army therefore became of the utmost importance and its loyalty was always unpredictable. Ecomonically, the reality again did not necessarily reflect theory. All land theoretically belonged to the king, to do with as he saw fit. Yet land actually was divided up into "royal" and "common" land. This common land in turn was divided into sacred, cleruchic, and gift land.[74] The division of land became quite hazy and obscure as military land-grants handed down from father to sons became generations removed from initial presentations. The kings constantly encroached on land not rightfully theirs (by practise, not theory).

As the two kingdoms continued on their courses, the base of power became viewed in different lights. The Ptolemies maintained a practise of the centralization of power. However, the Seleucids began to decentralize and allow for varying degrees of autonomy within their kingdom. One must remember that the king was still the

---

[74] V. Tcherikover, "The Hellenistic States", in A. Schalit, World History of the Jewish People, (1972), p. 23.

head of state, lawmaker, and grantor of this autonomy. His will created autonomy for three categories: cities, dynasts, and people; and all were still vassals of the king.[75]

Ever since the death of Alexander the Great, both Seleucid and Ptolemaic kingdoms sought to gain control of that "prized" land of Palestine. It initially fell into the hands of the Ptolemies in 301 BCE.[76] It had been the intention of Ptolemy I to go far to the north in his campaigns and conquer the whole of Syria.[77] However, he was forced simply to annex Palestine. The Zenon Papyri called the land "Syria and Phoenicia" and clearly define the limits of Ptolemiac control.[78]

10. PTOLEMY V EPIPHANES. Coin Portrait.

The situation radically changed in 205 BCE. Ptolemy IV Philopator died, and his son, the five year old Ptolemy V Epiphanes, ascended the throne. The advisors of young Ptolemy V rapidly gained control of the country. Riots and internal disorders were the order of the day as the kingship quickly lost its

---

[75] E. Bickerman, op. cit., pp.164-166.

[76] V. Tcherikover, "Palestine under the Ptolemies", Mitzraim 4-5 (1937).

[77] This can be assumed, based upon the reading of Diodorus XVIII, 43 and XIX, 57.

[78] PSI 324 and 495.

power and hold over the people. The first areas to suffer during this internal strife obviously were the outlying provinces. Palestine's Ptolemaic yoke was loosening, and Syria, under Antiochus III, felt that the time was ripe to fulfill Antiochus' dream of annexing southern Syria and Palestine for his own. In 201 BCE, he began his campaign and was quite successful, conquering nearly all of the terrotory, save the city of Gaza. Meanwhile, Egypt desperately wanted to reassert control, all the while attempting to put its own house in order. Ptolemy hired the Greek general, Scopas, to carry out his wishes.[79] The control of the land see-sawed back and forth until the Battle of Panion broke the Egyptian army's will. By 198 BCE., all of Palestine was frimly under the authority of the Seleucid Kingdom.[80]

The Status of Judea

As for Judea, Jerusalem, and the Jewish population, all three seem to have suffered enormously during this three year war. Polybius, via Josephus, described the nature of the see-saw battles that ravaged Judea.[81] The population was torn apart and forced to choose sides. It seems quite clear that factions within Judea supported both the Ptolemies and Seleucids. Heironymous, writing in the Fourth Century CE, described

---

[79] Josephus, AJ, XII, 130ff.

[80]   E. Bevan, House of Seleucus, pp. 300ff. and P.K.Hitti, History of Syria, p. 241f.

[81] Josephus, op. cit., 135 ff.

the situation rather accurately.[82] The rift within the
population appeared to follow social and economic lines
(supra.p.20ff)   Some scholars, such as Bevan, even
believe that the passage of Daniel 11:14 refers to this
turmoil.[83]

How did the indigenous Jewish population feel
towards the events that transpired in their land,
considering that, until the late 160's BCE, they would
be powerless to do anything much about it ? As Hengel
states, 'The remarkable thing is that the Jewish
judgements on the foreign state and its rulers in the
early Hellenistic Period are still overwhelmingly
positive.'[84] Some ancient authors believed that the role
of the Ptolemies was actually to upgrade Judea and bring
it into the modern world of the Hellenists. The Letter
of Aristeas as reported by Josephus is one such
example.[85] But this document originated in Alexandrian

---

[82]   Heironymous PL, vol 35 col., pp. 562f.
       "While the great Antiochus and
       Ptolemy's generals waged war
       between them, Judea, which lay
       in the middle, was drawn in two
       opposite directions; some supported
       Antiochus and the other Ptolemy."

[83]   E. Bevan, A Short Commentary on the Book of
Daniel, 1892. However, the difficulty with Daniel lies
in the dating of the book itself. Its date ranges from
the mid-Fifth Century BCE through the Second Century BCE.
Cf. J Slotkin, Daniel, Ezra, and Nehemiah, (1951), pp.91-
93 and Intro V, vi. Dan. 11-14,
       "In those times many shall rise against the King
       of the South; and the men of violence among your
       own people shall lift themselves up in order to
       fulfill the vision: but they shall fail."

[84]   M. Hengel, op. cit., p.29.

[85]   M. Hadas, Aristeas to Philocrates, (1951),p.54f.

Jewry, not Judean. Jews seemingly did play a more influential role under the Ptolemies in Egypt as members of the economy than did their counterparts in Judea, on the whole.[86] Daniel is perhaps another example of a somewhat positive Jewish view towards foreign control, in spite of the fact that the overall message in Daniel clearly is opposed to foreign domination. In general, Daniel gains favor and wins a high position in government.[87] In addition, the Prayer of Nabonidus illustrates a positive picture of a pagan king who converted to Judaism.[88] These views most likely "arose in the Hellenistic period and were probably first transmitted by word of mouth."[89] The generally favorable impression towards rule must have been created prior to the ascent of Antiochus IV, because all of his actions most certainly would have initiated a complete reversal of this approval (infra.p.80) Strong evidence to support this comes from decrees issued by Antiochus III himself. It is apparent that he desired a strong and useful province in Judea. To him, the only way to guarantee this was to have a stable situation politically, religiously, and economically. As is related to us in Josephus, a decree issued in Jerusalem in 198 BCE shows how he proposed to reward the Jewish population that helped in

---

[86] See Appendix One, CPJ 1 as an indication of Jewish roles in Egyptian affairs.

[87] Daniel 1-6.

[88] Daniel 4. Yet, at the same time, one must bear in mind that this only is true after Nabonidus has been thoroughly humiliated and has lost power.

[89] A. Bentzen in M. Hengel, op. cit., v.2,24, footnote 211.

the war; by rebuilding the city and suspending a variety of taxes.[90]   Ben Sirach seems to support the activities described in the decree of Antiochus III.[91]   Other works that also appear to have been written prior to the Antiochan persecutions, in this same literary genre, include Tobit,[92] Esther,[93] and III Ezra.[94]

It is evident that the awe and splendor of the Hellenistic state had its effect mainly on the upper strata of Jewish society (supra.p.35), but it must have filtered down to even the lowest segments of the population in one way or another. This openness and, to an extent, acceptance of the new ways by many was seen as both an asset and a detriment. The priestly class's fear of apostasy by the general population was always present and could easily manifest itself in many ways. Yet, on the other hand, even such anti-Hellenists as Ben Sirach saw some good in it all. The following refers to Jewish military service in the foreigner's occupying army:

> He serves among the great men and appears
> before rulers. He travels through the land of
> foreign nation and learns good and evil among
> men.[95]

---

[90]   Josephus _AJ_ XII, 138f.

[91]   Ben Sirach 50:1-2. LXX p.119.

[92] F. Zimmerman, "Thr Book of Tobit", in S. Zeitlin, ed., _Jewish Apocalyptic Literature_, 1958.

[93] S. Goldman, "Esther", in A. Cohen, ed., _The Five Megillot_, 1946.

[94] S. Sandmel, _Judaism and Christian Beginnings_, (1978), pp. 57-59.

[95]   Ben Sirach 39:4. LXX p. 108.

In the same breath, though, Ben Sirach warns against too much consorting with non-Jews:

> Receive a stranger in your house and he
> will alienate your way of thinking and
> he will estrange your family from you.[96]

Why does one see such a combination of mixed emotions ? As Gussman stated so aptly, "dread of the Greeks led to a wonderment at their success and at their power."[97]

A complete reversal in sympathies seems to come in the Second Century BCE, most probably a direct result of the rule of Antiochus IV. The respectful and benign attitudes of the Jews towards foreign rulers becomes hostile, if not downright vehement. Such works as Judith, [98] Additions to Esther, [99] or the works of III and IV Maccabees, [100] reflect this change. "Typical of this attitude is the maxim of Shemaiah, head of the Pharisaic school at the time of the last Hasmonean and Herod: 'Hate the dignity of the ruler and do not seek acquaintance with authority.'"[101] Finally, a passage out of Isaiah 9:10f in the Septuagint, dating from the Maccabean revolt or later sums up this reversal well:

---

[96] Ibid., 11:34. LXX, p. 84.

[97] H. Gussman in M. Hengel, op. cit., v.2, p. 25 footnote 228.

[98] E. Schurer, "Judith", Literature of the Jewish People at the Time of Jesus, (1887), pp. 33-37.

[99] Ibid., "Additions to Esther", pp. 181-183.

[100] S. Sandmel, op. cit., " III Maccabees", pp.265-267 and "IV Maccabees", pp. 277-279.

[101] Mishnah 'Aboth I, 10 b, in M. Hengel, op. cit., (1974), p. 30.

The bricks are fallen down, but come let us
hew stones, and cut down sycamores and cedars,
and let us build for ourselves a tower. And
God shall dash down them that shall rise up
against him on Mt. Zion, and shall scatter his
enemies: even Syria from the rising of the sun
who devour Israel, and the Greeks from the
setting of the sun...

versus the Hebrew version

The bricks are fallen but we will build with
hewn stones. The sycamores we will cut down
but cedars will be put in their place.
Therefore the Lord set upon high the
adversaries of Rezin against him: and spur
his enemies the Aramaeans on the east and the
Philistines on the west.[102]

---

[102] Isaiah 9:10-12 from The Septuagint Version of the
Old Testament, 1972, p. 844.

IV

EVENTS LEADING TO THE REVOLT

The series of events that finally serves to unify the entire Judean population in a revolt against Syria began in 168 BCE. For years, Antiochus IV attempted to play various factions of the Judean population off one another, courting many sides of a potentially volatile conflict at once. The priestly class was in turmoil, with its many different factions vying for power. Hellenization was at the root of all of the problems and Antiochus IV's meddling in internal affairs only worsened the situation.[103] Jerusalem became a Greek polis and the Jerusalemite aristocracy paved the way for Hellenistic reform in all areas of life save religion.[104] II Maccabees provides a good illustration of the tensions involved, as little sympathy is felt for supporters of this reform. Any changes would have surely incited revolt in the common people, yet none is described in the ancient sources. Official representation in the polis of Antioch-at-Jerusalem in no way wished to alter hundreds of years of religious

---

[103] V. Tcherikover, op. cit., (1959), p.392-395.

[104] E. Bickerman, Der Gott der Makkabaer, (1937), p. 63f. And also, V. Tcherikover, "Was Jerusalem a Polis ?", IEJ 14, (1964),p 61-78. Cf. I Macc., pp. 14-15.

tradition. This is made clear in II Maccabees 4:18;
discussing monetary offerings that were to be presented
to Heracles, not in sacrifice but for a building program.

Internal Politics

The Hellenizers came to an uneasy truce with
the High Priest, Jason, deciding that Jewish tradition
could indeed go hand in hand with Hellenism, thus opening
up Jerusalem to the outside world. This compromise
splintered the Hellenistic sympathizers, but not the
traditional population. The priestly class was split
from within, a conflict arising between the Tobiads and
the Oniads.[105] The outcome was that, for the first time,
someone not of the Oniad family of priests became the new
High Priest of Jerusalem. He was Menelaus, and the
reason for his appointment was chiefly due to the backing
of the Tobiad family; long an enemy of Jason and the
Oniads.[106] A new government was established, and within
this framework, the office of High Priest was suddenly
viewed as just another offical within the Seleucid
Empire, and would not necessarily be of ancestral
tradition; but rather bought and sold as any other
commodity typical of the Hellenistic era.[107]

Jerusalem suddenly reached the boiling point
and open battles raged in the streets. The rioters were
led by a group of leaders who called themselves Hasidim
and saw themselves as devoting their lives exclusively

---

[105] M. Hengel, op. cit., (1974), pp. 267-283.

[106] II Macc. 4:23-25.

[107] II Macc. 11:3.

to upholding the Torah. The impetus for this group's work came in 168 BCE, with the decree of Menelaus allowing the Temple treasury to be used for secular purposes.[108]

Seleucid Intervention

As the level of unrest grew, so too did the anger of Antiochus IV. Rome was heavily pressuring Antiochus to withdraw from Egypt, a humiliation that added to his frustration. His two campaigns, although somewhat successful, were doomed to ultimate failure by Rome's adamant stand in support of Egypt.[109] All of this was further inflamed by reports that other cities in Syria were also becoming areas of unrest. For example, Jerome writes that the city of Aradus in Phoenicia was also stirring up trouble for the Seleucids.[110] As a result, Antiochus IV believed that a firm hand was necessary in the case of Judea, to make a point for the rest of the kingdom.

11.ANTIOCHUS IV EPIPHANES. Coin portrait.

---

[108] V. Tcherikover, op. cit.,(1959),pp.155-157.

[109] Ibid., pp. 186-187. Note that the source of I Macc. 1:2 speaks of one campaign only in Egypt; yet II Macc. 5:11 and Daniel 11:28-30 have two.

[110] Jerome, On Daniel 11:44.

Antiochus IV apparently felt that it was essential to go directly to Jerusalem to confront his opponents, on the premise that the King's physical presence would serve as a great intimidating factor. It seems that this indeed is confirmed by the ancient sources themselves.[111] This "visit" brought with it a terrible massacre of people, as recorded in II Maccabees. It is stated that over 80,000 people were murdered during the three-day period.[112] However, an isolated attempt at suppression was not enough, and the city once again armed itself. At this time, the general Apollonius was dispatched by Antiochus IV himself to take political action to put down the revolt. The main source for these events is I Maccabees. II Maccabees is oddly silent on events that take place at this time. The people were not tricked into accepting Apollonius openly, as he had hoped, so he was forced to enter the city of Jerusalem on the premise of bringing an offer of peace for the king.[113]

Upon entering the city, Apollonius was compelled to use his mercenaries, the Moesians, and forcibly take the city on the Shabbat, indicating that it in fact was not previously held in Syria hands.[114] He

---

[111] See note 109 above.

[112] II Macc. 5:12ff. Bear in mind that all figures are often exaggerated for the sake of any cause; and that again one must be cautioned in the use of any text as an impeachable source.

[113] I Macc. 1:29f and II Macc. 5:24ff.

[114] V. Tcherikover, op. cit., (1959), p. 188. At times it is difficult to ascertain who does what; whether it be Antiochus IV or Apollonius. Cf. Josephus, AJ, XII, 247ff who attributes it all to Antiochus IV.

secured the city by
Hellenizing it with two
particularly repulsive
features that the Jews
could not tolerate: the
building of the Akra, or
citadel, in the center
of the polis; and the
establishing of his
Moesian troops as a
colony of foreign
soldiers, a **"katoikia"**

**12. MODEL OF THE HELLENISTIC
CITY OF JERUSALEM.**

or cleruchy, within the
heart of Jerusalem. As
was the case quite often in the Graeco-Roman world, the
establishment of a Katoikia in most instances led to the
destruction of the indigenous community.[115]

The end result was a mass exodus from
Jerusalem, leaving it in the hands of the foreigners.[116]
Although some scholars refer to the account of I
Maccabees as "pure fantasy,[117] a majority feel that, based
on the decrees of Apollonius, the flight was wholly
justifiable. The Katoikia involved not merely the
installation of troops, but legalized robbery,
confiscation of land, murder, etc. In addition, the

---

115 Perhaps this act is what is referred to in Daniel
11:39 and certainly in I Macc. 1:35-38 and 3:45.

116 I Macc. 1:38ff.

117 J.S. Dancy, A Commentary on I Maccabees, 1954,
p. 73. Similarly, see J. Goldstein, I Maccabees, 1976,
p. 212-215.

Temple of Jerusalem also appears to have been desecrated by Apollonius.[118]

The Rise of the Hasidim

Following this mass flight and persecution, the Hasidim began to organize into a fighting group. These "freedom fighters" were already in operation long before the Hasmoneans made their entrance on the political and military scene. The Book of Daniel clearly indicates that there were leaders of an insurrection prior to Judah Maccabees, and acknowledges that suffering and persecution were common to them.[119] These Hasidim saw themselves as loyal exclusively to the Torah and its precepts. In fact, they even refused to fight on the Shabbat and preferred death to a profanation of the Law.[120] However, their religious zeal did not appear to extend to foolishness and unnecessary martyrdom. Eventually, with the rise of the Hasmoneans, a great number of Hasidim joined to present a united front against the common enemy,[121] in spite of the fact that Daniel continues to paint a more passive picture,

---

[118] I Macc. 1:39. The author of Maccabees places the events prior to Antiochus IV's persecutions, and there is not enough evidence to doubt that the Temple of Jerusalem was not desecrated twice.

[119] Daniel 11:33f.

[120] I Macc. 2:31ff.

[121] I Macc. 2:40-42.

expecting divine intervention against Antiochus IV.[122]
That they would join a group such as the Maccabees proved
that the Hasidim realized when to bend the law for a
greater good.

In light of this information, another approach
must be taken when viewing the Jewish rebellion. A
majority of scholars previously had used the primary
sources to construct a relative chronology of the revolt.
According to the Maccabees' account, the uprising took
place based on the following sequence of events: 1)
internal conflicts within the Jewish population; 2)
military intervention by Antiochus IV in Judea; 3)
Antiochus IV's persecutions; 4) the Hasmonean rebellion.
Therefore, rebellion came as a direct result of the
Antiochan persecutions. However, Bickerman, Tcherikover
and others questioned the nature of Antiochan
persecutions. It is generally agreed that religious
persecution was virtually unknown, and that the
Hellenistic culture was highly tolerant vis-a'-vis local
religions within the empire.[123] Eastern cults were never
abolished; rather, a syncretistic approach was used. As
a result, the order of events should perhaps be altered
or expanded to be more accurate as follows: 1) internal
conflicts within the Jewish community; 2) attempts by
Antiochus IV to strengthen the southern portion of his
kingdom; 3)revolt by the Hasidim; 4) persecution by
Antiochus IV; 5) Hasmonean revolt.[124]

---

[122]   G.W.E. Nicklesburg, 1981, p. 83ff: after J.J.
Collins, Apocalyptic Vision of the Book of Daniel, 1979,
pp. 95-152.

[123]   E. Bickerman, op. cit.,(1937), p.117.

[124]   V. Tcherikover, op. cit.,(1959), p. 191.

One other theory, that of Bickerman, is worth noting with regard to the Hellenized Jewish community. As Hengel points out, the consecration of the Temple to Zeus[125] cannot be viewed as initiative of Antiochus IV with regard to his "Hellenization policy".[126] Neither can the above mentioned view of Tcherikover be considered fully accurate. It can be asked why this rebellion, in the earliest stages, could not have been put down in the usual manner; ie. with force, rather than through clamping down on the religion of those involved. Bickerman, therefore, proposed that it was the Hellenized Jews themselves who were primarily responsible for inciting, or escalating of the events in Judea prior to the Hasmonean revolt.[127] He believed that the literature supports this, in both Daniel and Maccabees. For instance, in Daniel one reads, "He will make strong a covenant for the many, a week (of years) long."[128] It is assumed that this refers to a pact between the king and the Hellenists. This would fit in well with the rule of the High Priest Menelaus, from 172-165 BCE, or "a week of years", seven years. Josephus adds to this theory in stating that the Tobiads, supporters of Menelaus, wished to "abandon their ancestral laws and the way of life prescribed in them, and to follow the royal laws and adopt the Greek way of life."[129] Finally, Josephus adds

---

[125] I Macc. 1:44f and II Macc. 6:1ff

[126] M. Hengel, op. cit.,(1974),p. 287.

[127] E. Bickerman, op. cit.,(1937), p. 120ff.

[128] Daniel 9:27.

[129] Josephus, AJ, XII,241. Cf. also I Macc. 1:11f.

the following, seemingly to clinch the arguments to the
extreme role of the Hellenists and Menelaus:

> That he (Antiochus V) should kill
> Menelaus if he wanted to give the
> Jews peace and not   make any more
> trouble for himself, as Menelaus had
> caused the disturbance by convincing
> his father (Antiochus IV) to compel
> the Jews to give up their traditional
> worship of God. [130]

---

[130] Ibid., XII,384ff; and also a similar account is
in II Macc. 13:3f.   This seems to add to the basic
credibility of this account.

V

THE PERSECUTIONS

In the winter of the year immediately following the suppressions of Apollonius, 167/6 BCE, the **"Gezerot"**, persecutions of Antiochus IV, were enacted. Again, I and II Maccabees are the most important primary sources. However, their accounts remain fairly general and do not provide many details. There may once have been a more detailed account prepared by Jason of Cyrene; however, this appears to be lost to us.[131]

The Account of I Maccabees

I Maccabees gives a reasonable description of the Antiochan persecutions, but doubts have been raised as to the validity or accuracy of this report. The common argument is that propaganda and the use of exaggerated accounts go hand in hand when trying to espouse a particular cause, or support a people or movement. The argument stems from a passage that paints a picture of Antiochus IV as a Hellenizer and religious unifier.[132] Here, it is stated that Antiochus IV sent a message to the population of the entire empire calling for a "covenant with the nations that are around us: for

---

[131] M. Hengel, op. cit., (1972), p. 139.

[132] I Macc. 1:10-16.

come upon us."[133] However, there is really no substantial evidence for the historicity of this decree. Tcherikover believes it to be the view of the author of I Maccabees that the persecutions were a part of a greater religious reform throughout the Seleucid Empire.[134] On the other hand, scholars such as Dancy and Bickerman believe it to be merely pure fiction.[135] Goldstein approaches the passage as a "scene-setting" block of text designed to set the stage for the remainder of the narrative.[136]

Regardless of the introductory passage, the description of the persecution as related in I Macc.1:44-51 appears to be more reliable. It is revealed that the customs of foreign religion--that is, Greek and Syrian cults-- were to be practised by the Jews. The abolition of Jewish religious activities was to accompany this, such as the cessation of burnt offerings and all forms of sacrifice. The Shabbat and other feast days were to be profaned, and the sanctuary in Jerusalem to be blasphemed. In addition, the establishment of centers for these foreign cults was to be carried out; building high places and sacred groves. The final insult was of major significance; that of prohibiting the rite of circumcision. In essence, this was a direct order that would symbolically and physically break the covenant that

---

[133]   I Macc. 1:11b.

[134]   V. Tcherikover, op. cit.,(1959),p.39.

[135]   J.S.Dancy, op. cit.,(1954),p. 75 and E. Bickerman, op. cit.,(1937), pp. 127f.

[136]   J. Goldstein, op. cit.,(1976), p.. 190-193.

God made with Abraham,[137] and Moses.[138] Whoever, did not abide by these decrees faced death.

The major act of violence and persecution that befell Judea and the Jews came on the 15th of Kislev, 167 BCE. The account of I Maccabees 1:54ff described it as "an abomination of desolation", set upon the altar in the Temple of Jerusalem. Coupled with his desecration, Torah scrolls were burnt and the death penalty invoked for hiding them.[139] Officials were even appointed to make sure that these orders were carried out. It is a certainty that these orders were designed not only for Jerusalem, but all of the other towns of Judea as well.[140] The account continues with the offering of a "polluted"

13. ANTIOCHUS IV COMMANDING THE SLAUGHTER OF THE INHABITANTS OF JERUSALEM. 16TH Century Illuminated French Manuscript.

---

[137] Genesis 17:9-11.

[138] Exodus 4:24-26.

[139] I Macc. 1:44f.

[140] V. Tcherikover, op. cit.,(1959), p. 196. See also II Macc. 6:8; "... a decree was issued to neighboring cities, commanding them to impose the same manner of observance and participation in the sacrifice upon the Jews...".

sacrifice ten days later on the same altar. The
identical episodes are also mentioned in <u>Daniel</u>.[141]

14. I MACCABEES 2:49-3:11. Codex Sinaiticus. 4th
Century.

---

[141]   <u>Daniel</u> 11:31.

The Account of II Maccabees

The account as described in II Maccabees adds further information. According to the narrative, the Jews were not only prohibited from performing ritual, but subject to the "compelling" by a special envoy to abandon Judaism.[142] The Greek text says that this person was **"Geronte Athenaion"**, and most scholarship believes this to refer to "an elder of Athens", who served in this capacity.[143] With regard to the desecration of the Temple in Jerusalem, II Maccabees goes on to state that the structure was then rededicated to Zeus Olympus and turned over to the "goyim". who brought in temple prostitutes for "riot and revelling".[144] In addition, similar events took place, most notably on the temple at Mt. Gerizim.[145] It was forbidden to keep the Shabbat and all other festivals. In their stead, the population was required to celebrate the birthday of Antiochus IV each month by the offering of sacrifices in honor of Dionysius.

An interesting passage claims that it was forbidden to "openly confess oneself to be a Jew."[146] in the parallel account of I Macc. 1:44-51. This reveals clearly how the population was viewed from afar, as the

---

[142] II Macc, 6:1.

[143] S. Zeitlin, The Second Book of Maccabees, 1954, p. 151.

[144] I. and L. Robert, "Bulletin Epigraphique", REG 64, (1951), p.130.

[145] II Macc. 6:1b-5.

[146] Ibid., 6:6. However, the possibility arises that this passage could have been an addition by the author of II Maccabees.

book was written in Antioch. The Jewish population in
Antioch were called "Hebrews" of the Judean-Jewish
religion; while those in Judea were called Judeans, or
Jews. Therefore, the implication is that the term "Jews"
was strictly a religious one, and that the prohibition
was solely aimed at anyone calling himself a Jew in the
religious sense of the word.[147] To illustrate the
persecutions and place them on a more meaningful,
personal level, II Maccabees 6-7 concludes with examples
of cruelty and executions; thus singling out and
martyring a few "heroes".

---

[147] S. Zeitlin, op. cit.,(1954), p.152-153.

The Scope of the Persecutions

The above descriptions reveal the end results of the decrees of Antiochus IV, and the punishments associated with them, but what did the repressive decrees really entail? The cornerstone of all of these decrees was the basic abolition of the rights of Jews to live religiously acording to his/her ancestral traditions. Coupled with this was the attempt to impose Greek customs on the local population. The above rationale has formed the basis of Bickerman's view of affording a legal foundation for the abolishing of the rights of the Jew that had previously been granted by Antiochus III (supra.p.72) and as a means of initiating the first steps of a sweeping Hellenization movement.[148] Since the "religious freedom act" of Antiochus III had already been rescinded by Antiochus IV in 175 BCE, when the polis of Antioch-at-Jerusalem was established by the High Priest Jason, this theory lacks strong support.[149] At this time, nothing was in reality abolished; rather, Hellenistic customs were simply added to the previous decrees.

---

[148] E. Bickerman, op. cit., (1937), p.117-118.

[149] For the decree, see V. Tcherikover, op. cit., (1959), pp. 125-126. For more on the abolition, see M. Hengel, op. cit., (1974), p. 278f.

Therefore, it seems that the Jewish Hellenizing movement's activities cannot really be held responsible for the rise in religious persecution against the more traditional Jewish community; only the king himself.[150] These decrees of Antiochus IV were official documents published as an official order, **"a Prostagma"**, and were designed to restore loyalty to Judea, while at the same time, suppressing and outlawing the religious cult. Because of his actions, Antiochus IV Epiphanes effectively short-circuited the previously important role of the Hellenizing Jewish community. In other words, the only intermediary party that stood in the way of the Seleucid Empire and the Judean traditionalists was gone from the arena. With the buffer no longer in place, the way was clear for the ensuing conflict.

---

[150] Bear in mind, again, that this rescinding of an earlier law by the King wasn't deemed illegal, nor needed the approval of the Gerousia, as the King was the law and didn't require counsel.

15. SELEUCID WAR ELEPHANT. Medallion. [Villa Giulia, Rome]

The True Goals of the Actions

If the aim of the decrees per se was not to abolish the Jewish religion, what **were** the main goals? Persecution of the traditional practises of Judaism was certainly a goal, but only as a means of suppressing the politics of the rebels. It was felt that, if the Torah was abolished, the rebels would lose their source of inspiration. A second goal obviously was the imposition of more Greek customs on the population. Since many customs had already taken root in the Jerusalem community under the leadership of Jason (supra.), Antiochus felt that most of the masses would simply continue to accept more reforms; epecially in light of the fact that the Jews themselves had previously initiated the first actions of Hellenization. Apparently, he also felt that, with the destruction of Judaism, the resulting vacuum would naturally be filled by the Hellenistic cult. However, as has occurred on numerous occasions, assimilation and syncretism have often been rejected by Judaism after prolonged temptation and struggle and this was especially evident at this stage.[151] And, as a result, these acts only encouraged the "fixed intellectual development of the Torah."[152]

Finally, with regard to the level of cruelty described in the decrees of persecution, one finds that the sources lay particular stress on the king's personal involvement. It appears that a deliberate attempt by the authors of both I and II Maccabees is made to show hatred of the Seleucids for a rebellious people on one hand, and

---

[151] M. Hengel, op. cit.,(1974), p.308.

[152] Ibid., p. 308.

the religious fanaticism of a people turned to political action on the other. Consequently, one cannot necessarily take the sources at face value with regard to the king's actual participation. An indication of this participation is the episode in II Maccabees where the king presided over some of the tortures personally.[153] These are seen purely as legend used initially to strengthen the

16. SELEUCID WAR ELEPHANT. [On vase (Villa Giulia, Rome)]

rebels' morale. In actuality, at the time of these supposed occurrences, Antiochus IV was preparing to leave Syria to deal with the Parthians in an attempt to put down rebellion flaring in the East. Here, he ultimately met his end.[154] However, the goals of II and IV Maccabees appear to have backfired, in that the aspects of Antiochus IV as an "anti-semite" (anti-Jew), eventually led to his being " a political model of the new anti-semitism."[155] Several ancient authors discuss his actions and interpret them in that fashion, and apparently all of this "press" on his supposed deeds led to the actions

---

[153] II Macc. 7 and later IV Macc. 8-18.

[154] W. Tarn, op. cit. (1952), p. 34f.

[155] M. Hengel, op. cit., (1974), p. 306f.

by later Roman emperors, according to Bickerman.[156] This
is supported as well in later scholarship by Goldstein.[157]

---

[156] E. Bickerman, op. cit.,(1937), p. 21ff. These
other ancient authors included Posidonius, via Diodorus
44fr.1; Apion, via Josephus, Contra Apion 2,80f;
Porphyry, Against the Christians; Jerome, On Daniel;
Tacitus, Histories 5,8,2.

[157] J. Goldstein, op. cit., (1976), p. 159ff.

VI.

REBELLION OR REVOLUTION

          After having examined the social, political,
religious and economic background for the Hasmonean
uprising, one needs to place it within the context of
their events. As Burridge stated, religion deals with
the systematic order of power. In other words, religious
activity is closely bound to every facet of the human
condition. As a result, "no religion lacks a political
ideology."[1] In this respect, millenary movements within
a religion are rooted in the execution of traditional
values. If these traditional values collapse, then the
rebellious political movement is born and rapidly gains
momentum. In essence it is a protest movement that
seizes power.[2] As Sorokin states, mand is made up of a
number of instincts based on wants and needs: "...the
need for food; the instinct for individual or collective
self-preservation;...property-owning instinct; desire to
be recognized...."[3] It is the disintegration of these
values that allows for creation and frequently success
of the millenary movement.

          Why do these values collapse ? It seems evident
that several causes share in this collapse: colonialism,

---

[1] K. Burridge, New Heaven, New Earth, 1969, p. 7.

[2] J. Baechler, Revolution, 1975, p. 91.

[3] Ibid., p.7.

imbalance of power, breakdown of traditional prestige systems, and an introduction of money; thereby leading to disassociation from the social and natural world. All of these lead to the motives as outlined by Baechler of 1) hatred for the occupying force, 2) humiliation, 3) despair, 4) fear, 5) oppression, 6) envy, and 7) rejection of incompetence.[4]   What are found are a combination of both endogenous and exogenous political/religious movements. Ofttimes, these movements will then form a united front in order to deal successfully with the external opposing force and further their agendas.   This is clearly in evidence in the Hasmonean uprising.   This idea is closely akin to Burridge's theory regarding the general pattern of the development of millenary movements.   The first step is disenfranchisement, when the knowledge of separation is realized.   The value of the "shared experience" of the human condition is drastically reduced, creating and enhancing the need to fall back on ones' own resources.[5]

The second phase, as seen by Burridge, is the externalization of thoughts and ideas. Attempts are made to express actively solutions to the problems besetting the people.   Ofttimes it is syncretistic, blending the best of several traditions for this outward expression.[6] Again, with the Hasmonean movement, several traditions are gathered within the all-encompassing umbrella of the priestly family from Modi'in; whether it be Hasidic religious or disenchanted villagers overcome by the

---

[4]   Ibid., p. 94-95.

[5]   Burridge, op. cit., (1969), p. 105f.

[6]   Ibid., p. 107f.

"modernization" of the Hellenistic world. This is seen by Baechler as being rather limited due to the nature of the millenary movement.[7] Infighting in the Hellenistic world clearly opened the door in this case. This brings one to Burridge's third phase, that of the aftermath. Sometimes the movement is victorious and change is instituted. Other times, sects develop and survive on a limited scale.[8] However, most of the time the movement fails and this failure will start the cycle all over again.[9] The Hasmoneans failed through their own human fallibility, which allowed for internal decay. This concept also fits in well with Baechler's last two groups of reformers, based on Weber's typology, of counter-societies and true revolutionaries.[10]

Another question to be resolved, based on the data presented, is whether the uprising is a rebellion or revolution. According to Hobsbawn, one can't possibly have a revolution prior to the American Revolution of 1776. Only rebellion, in Hobsbawn's terms, is possible.[168] It appears that, to him, the difference is only the degree of consciousness between the two classifications. He states the differences clearly by "their acceptance or not of the general framework of the institution or social arrangement."[169] This is fully

---

[7] Baechler, op. cit.,(1975), p. 83ff.

[8] Ibid., p. 36.

[9] Burridge, op. cit.,(1969) p. 112.

[10] Baechler, op. cit., (1975), p.44.

[168] E.J.Hobsbawn, Primitive Rebels, 1959, pp. 58-59.

[169] Ibid., p. 58-59.

explored in Chapter IV of Hobsbawn, but in essence can be reduced to the following simplified comparison.

Rebels and revolutionaries have a number of similar points between them. Both groups see a need for change within their respective societies. The basic reason seen for this change is the fact that an inordinate amount of human suffering has taken place at the hands of the ruling party or parties. Changes are needed because of the growing dissatisfaction with the status quo. Social injustice is perceived as becoming more rampant, as the ruling power disenfranchises itself from the general populace. Attempts at change using the existing social channels or apparatus have failed miserably or have been seen as being futile attempts from the outset. As a result, the only avenue left to both the revolutionaries and rebels is the use of violence in order to exact the changes that they deem necessary. However, at this point, the similarity between the two groups ends, and their ultimate philosophies crystallize into clear-cut differentiations as follows.

In a rebellion, one seemingly will respond to the superficial symptoms of a decaying society. Deeper ills are not considered because this would require the development of an ideological basis for all actions. Rebellion lacks this ideological basis. As a result, activities are severely limited and never grow from its small scale origins. The narrowness of viewpoint and limited base of operations inevitably leads to a distinct lack of both an organization and set of effective tactics. An outgrowth of this absence of guidance is seen via the rebellious group's unrealistic and most likely unattainable goals.[170]

On the other hand, revolution appears to be a much more serious business. The revolutionary understands or seems to grasp the myriad problems that confront his/her society, and therefore attempt to develop a response to the in-depth disease tht afflicts the society. Out of this response comes an ideology based on eradicating those problems. This cannot be accomplished on a small scale, so the revolutionary creates a massive base of operations that cuts through economic, social, and apparently religious strata in society. Through an efficient, highly organized network, effective tactics are developed and incorporated into the overall strategies. Finally, the revolution is able to come to terms with what it can and cannot do in a fairly impartial manner. The goals that are strived for are realistic goals. However, they are extremely ambitious ones that may prove to be difficult, yet not impossible, to achieve.[171]

All of this appears to fit with Baechler's idea of the nature of a peasant war.[172] However, based on the simplified analysis of Hobsbawn regarding revolution and rebellion, one is forced to disagree with Baechler concerning the pro forma categorization of the Hasmonean uprising as merely a rebellion. The earliest phase of discontent in the 160's-150's BCE may have had all of the qualifications of rebellion, but that this rapidly

---

[170]   Cf. Baechler, op. cit.,(1975) pp. 94-95 as a response to the collapse of values.

[171]   Ibid., p. 94-95.

[172]   Baechler, op. cit., (1975), p. 51-54.

changed with the rise of Simon, the Hasmonean; and his sons in the 140's, and their rather highly developed organization. Their discipline and organizational commitment and ideology succeeded in the re-establishment of a Jewish kingdom after some 400 years.

This argument, however, is precisely the problem that is posed to us. How, then, can the re-establishment of anything be regarded as something revolutionary. Would it not be implied that this is merely a reversion to the status quo and restoration of a previous concept or regime in this case ? The simple label of "Jewish Kingdom" does not necessarily imply a reversion to the Kingdom of Israel during the Monarchial Era (1060-587 BCE). The nature of that state, its culture, economics, politics, and spirituality are far removed from the nature of that of the Hasmoneans. Rather, the phrase should be viewed as an identification of a body of people descended from a particular cultural and religious background- taking those necessary steps involved in the ongoing process of evolution, people-making, that allows for constant growth and renewal.[173] The religion of the Hellenistic Jewish World, although founded on the same basic concepts of Law and Covenant, was syncretistic, "modernized", evolved from its conceptualization hundreds of years earlier. The economic and social order, too, had evolved as well. So one is not inclined, cannot be inclined, to consider this movement as counter-revoultionary, rebellious, or even restorative; but rather a true revolution, with the same results.

---

[173] In much the same way, one can't identify the former Shah of Iran with the Persian Empire of the 6th-5th Centuries BCE.

As Baechler implies, the functions of revolution are to 1) disrupt the social equilibrium, 2) restore equilibrium, and 3) establish a new equilibrium.[174] The protest movement, as stated before, does seize power and initiate a new order of things. The main task seen is to re-organize, using traditional sources of authority.[175] After all, when one considers the root of the word **protest** one can more clearly understand this role. **Protest** comes from the Latin **Protestari**, which can mean both **to protest against** or **to affirm**. In this light, the revolution of the Hasmoneans and the re-establishment of a Jewish state actually is able to do both at the same time.

16. JUDAH THE MACCABEE. French Enamel Medallion. 16th Century.

These occurrences within the Hasmonean movement succeeded for many decades in re-creating a new order. However, a combination of internal and external forces brought about the downfall of this kingdom, and it would not be for another 2100 years that a Jewish State is re-established again in the geographical region of Syria/Palestine.

---

[174] Baechler, op. cit., (1975), p. 38ff.

[175] Burridge, op. cit., (1969), p.79-83.

APPENDIX ONE
THE ZENON PAPYRI

VII

APPENDIX ONE

THE ZENON PAPYRI

The following translations of the Zenon Papyri are all taken from V. Tcherikover and A. Fuks, Corpus Papyrorum Judaicarum I, 1957. pp. 118-130.

CPJ 1

In the 27th year of the
reign of Ptolemy, son of Ptolemy, and of
his son Ptolemy, the priest of Alexander
and of the gods Adelphoi and the
kanephoros of Arsinoe Philadelphos being
those in office in Alexandria, in the
month Zandikos, at Birta of the
Ammanitis. Nicanor, son of
Xenokles, Knidian, in the service
of Toubias, sold Zenon
son of Agrephon Kaunian,
in the service of Apollonius
the dioketes, a Sidonian girl
named Sphragis, about
seven years of age, for
fifty drachmai.
Guarantor... son of
Ananias, Persian, of the
troop of Toubias,
kleruch.
Witnesses:...judge; [...

son of Agathon] Persian
(cancelled) Polemon son of
Straton, Macedonian, of the cavalrymen
of Toubias, kleruch; Timopolis son of
Botes, Milesian; Heraklitos son of
Phillipos, Athenian; Zenon son of
Timarchos,Kolophonian; Demostratos son
of Dionysios, Aspendian; all four in the
service of Apollonios, the dioketes.
[Endorsed] deed of sale of a girl.

CPJ 2a   flour

In Straton's tower	5 artabai
Jerusalem	6
In Jericho	5
In Abella	3
Surabit...	9 artabai
Lakasa	14
Noe	10
Eitoui	7
Baitianata	14
Kydisos	2
In Ptolemais	4

CPJ 2b
Philemon the baker
Lamedon
In Jerusalem wheat-flour   2 artabai
from Toubias   1 artabe
to...   1 3/4 artabai

CPJ 2c
To Toubias' donkeys
To Toubias' 3 horses

CPJ 2d
Col.iii,1.17:
 to the grooms of Toubias:1 Xous
Col.ix,11.10-16
28th in Abella
for the men's apartment:1 keration
to the servants have been distributed...
to Artemidoros   (3 kotylai)
In Sorabit...

CPJ 2e
Col.3
From Sidon into Galilee carrying
 grain they received   48 drachmai
For another grain transport from the same
place   48 drachmai
With Simon, from Galilee, carrying
 grain   150 drachmai

CPJ 3

> Hippostratos,Auelos,
> Panabelos, Zabalnos, Philon
> Menon, Zenon, Hosaios, Annaios(cancel),
> Sanaios, Koustanos, Nikon,
> Pr...

CPJ 4

> Toubias to Apollonios
> greeting. If you and all your affairs
> are flourishing, and everything else is
> as you wish it, many thanks to
> the gods ! I too have been well, and
> have thought of you at all times, as was
> right.

CPJ 4

> I have sent to you Aineias bringing a
> eunuch and four boys,house-slaves and of
> good stock, two of whom are
> uncircumcised. I append descriptions of
> the boys for your information
> Goodbye   Year 29, Xandikos 10.

Haimos. About 10	Atikos. About 8
Dark skin	Light skin
Curly hair	Curly hair
Black eyes	Nose somewhat flat
Rather big jaws	Black eyes, scar
with moles on	the right eye
the right jaw	
Uncircumcised	Uncircumcised

Audomos. About 10   Okaimos. About 7
Black eyes   Round face
Curly hair   Nose flat
 Nose flat   Grey eyes
Protruding lips   Fiery complexion
Scar near right   Long straight hair
 eyebrow   Scar on forehead
Circumcised   above right
                            eyebrow
                           Circumcised

(addressed) to Apollonios
(docketed) Toubias, about a eunuch and
4 boys he has sent. Year 29,
Artemesion 16, at Alexandria.

CPJ 5   To King Ptolemy from Toubias,greetings.
               I have sent you two horses, six dogs,
               one wild mule out of an ass, two white
               Arab donkeys, two wild mules' foals and
               one wild ass's foal
                  Farewell.
               (addressed) to Apollonios.
               (docketed) Toubias, about hisconsignment
               to the King, and the copy of his
               letter to the King. Year 29, 16
          Artemesion, at Alexandria.

CPJ 5   Toubias to Apollonios greeting. On the
                10th of Xandikos I sent Aineias our
                servant, bringing the gifts for the King
                which you wrote and asked me to send in
                the month of Xandikos:2 horses, 6 dogs,
                1 wild mule out of an ass, 2 white Arab
                donkeys, 2 wild mule's foals, 1 wild
                ass's foal. They are all tame. I have
                also sent you the letter which I have
                written to the King about the gifts,
                together with a copy for your
                information.
                Goodbye.   Year 29, Xandikos 10.

CPJ 6   [Alexan]dros to Oryas, greeting. I have
                received your letter, to which you added
                a copy of the letter written by Zenon to
                Jedous saying that unless he gave the
                money to Straton, Zenon's man, we were
                to hand over his pledge to him(Straton).
                I happened to be unwell as a result of
                taking some medecine so I sent a lad, a
                servant of mine, with Straton, and wrote
                a letter to Jedous. When they had
                returned they said that he had taken
                no notice of my letter, but had attacked
                them and thrown them out of the village.
                So I am writing to you (for your
                information).

                Goodbye. Year 27, Peritios intercalary 20
                (addressed to) Oryas.

The following translation is taken from C.C.Edgar,
Zenon Papyri, Cairo.

PCZ 59093   Apollophanes also has arrived in Syria
             and on our expedition to Massyas we have
             met him at Sidon and told him that Krotos
             is waiting in Joppa for an opportunity
             of exporting... and mattresses. He
             replied that he could not sail there
             at present, for he had been ordered by
             Dionysodoros to bring his bags to
             Herakleia. He informed us too that those
             at home were all well. And Menekles of
             Tyre, he said, had brought some slaves
             and merchandise from Gaza to Tyre and
             landed them in Tyre for transshipment
             without notifying the customs officers
             and without having a permit to export
             slaves, and on learning this they had
             taken them from him. So Apollonios
             coming to the aid of Menekles
           declared that the slaves and the
             merchandise were yours, and Menekles
             obliged to back him up.

APPENDIX TWO
MAPS

VIII

APPENDIX TWO

MAPS

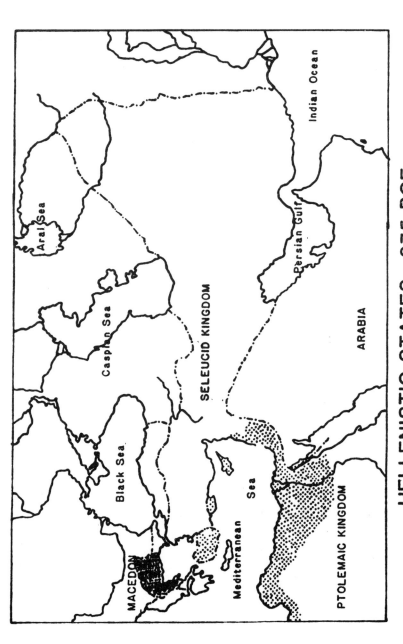

HELLENISTIC STATES– 275 BCE

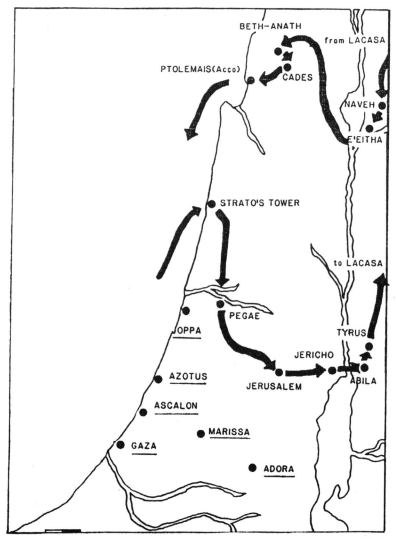

TRAVELS OF ZENON IN PALESTINE- 259/8 BCE

Azotus- city with Zenon's agent

PALESTINE UNDER THE PTOLEMIES AND SELEUCIDS

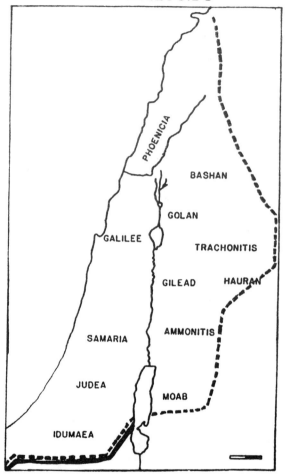

FRONTIER OF PTOLEMAIC DOMAIN–pre 198 BCE ··

FRONTIER BETWEEN THE TWO STATES–
post 198 BCE

EXPANSION OF THE
HASMONEAN STATE

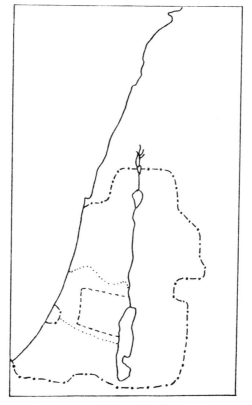

JERUSALEM TERRITORY 167 BCE

CONQUESTS of SIMON 140 BCE

CONQUESTS of ALEXANDER
JANNAI 76 BCE ─.─.─.

APPENDIX THREE
DYNASTIC LISTS

IX

APPENDIX THREE

DYNASTIC LISTS

The Seleucid Dynasty of Syria *

Seleucus I Nicator	311–281 BCE
Antiochus I Soter	281–261 BCE
Antiochus II Theos	261–246 BCE
Seleucus II Callinicus	246–225 BCE
Seleucus III Soter	225–223 BCE
Antiochus III the Great	223–187 BCE
Seleucus IV Philopater	187–175 BCE
Antiochus IV Epiphanes	175–164 BCE
Antiochus V Eupator	163–162 BCE
Demetrius I Soter	162–150 BCE
Alexander Balas	150–145 BCE
Demetrius II Nicator	145–140 BCE
Antiochus VI Epiphanes	145–138 BCE
Antiochus VII Sidetes	138–129 BCE
Demetrius II Nicator	129–125 BCE
Cleopatra Thea	126 BCE
Cleopatra Thea and Antiochus VIII Grypus	125–121 BCE
Seleucus V	125 BCE
Antiochus VI Grypus	121–96 BCE
Antiochus IX Cyzicencus	115–95 BCE
Seleucus VI Epiphanes Nicator	96–95 BCE
Demetrius III Philopater	95–88 BCE
Antiochus X Eusebes	95–83 BCE
Antiochus XI Philadelphus	94 BCE

Philip I Philadelphus	94-83 BCE
Antiochus XII Dionysius	87-84 BCE
Antiochus XIII	69-64 BCE
Philip II	67-65 BCE*

overlapping dates = co-regencies

The Ptolemaic Dynasty of Egypt *

```
Ptolemy I Soter                       304-282 BCE
Ptolemy II Philadelphus               282-246 BCE
Ptolemy III Euergetes                 246-221 BCE
Ptolemy IV Philopator                 221-204 BCE
Ptolemy V Epiphanes                   204-180 BCE
Ptolemy VI Philometor                 180-145 BCE
Ptolemy VII Neos Philopator           145-144 BCE
Ptolemy VIII Euergetes II             145-116 BCE
Ptolemy IX Soter II                   116-107 BCE
Ptolemy X Alexander I                 107-88 BCE
Ptolemy IX Soter II (restored)        88-81 BCE
Ptolemy XI Alexander II               80 BCE
Ptolemy XII Neos Dionysios            80-51 BCE
Cleopatra VII Philopator              51-30 BCE
Ptolemy XIII                          51-47 BCE
Ptolemy XIV                           47-44 BCE
Ptolemy XV                            44-30 BCE
```

* Overlapping dates = co-regencies

The Maccabean Dynasty

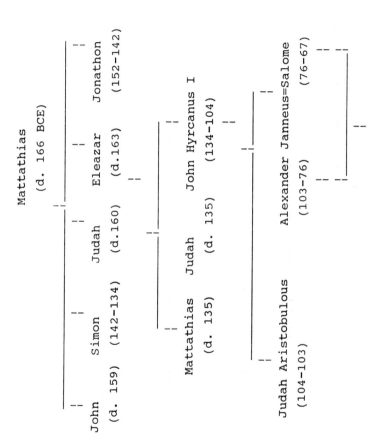

Mattathias
(d. 166 BCE)

John   Simon   Judah   Eleazar   Jonathon
(d. 159)   (142-134)   (d.160)   (d.163)   (152-142)

Mattathias   Judah   John Hyrcanus I
(d. 135)   (d. 135)   (134-104)

Judah Aristobulous   Alexander Janneus=Salome
(104-103)   (103-76)   (76-67)

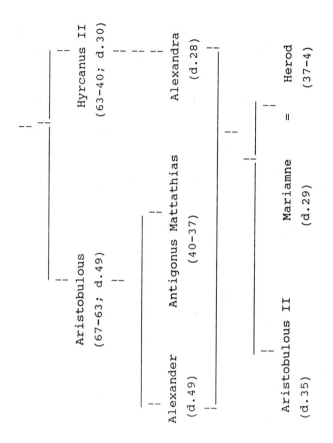

BIBLIOGRAPHY

Abel, F.M., "La liste geographique du papyrus 71 de
       Zenon", <u>RB</u> 32, 1923.

Aharoni, Y., <u>Excavations at Ramat Rachel</u>, Rome:
       University of Rome, 1964.

_____, <u>Land of the Bible</u>, Philadelphia:
       Westminster, 1967a.

_____, "Tel Beersheva:Notes and News", <u>IEJ</u> 17.4,
       1967b.

_____, "The Arad Temple", <u>BA</u> 31.1, 1968a.

_____, "The Israelite Sanctuary at Arad", <u>NDBA,</u>
       Garden City: Doubleday, 1971.

_____, "Excavations at Tel Beersheva", <u>TA</u> 1.1,
       1972a.

_____, "Tel Beersheva:Notes and News", <u>IEJ</u> 22.2-3,
       1972b.

_____, <u>Beersheva I</u>, Ramat Aviv:Tel Aviv
       University, 1973a.

_____, "Tel Beersheva:Notes and News", <u>IEJ</u> 23.4,
       1973b.

_____, <u>Lachish V</u>, Ramat Aviv: Tel Aviv
       University, 1975a.

_____, "Excavations at Tel Beersheva 1973-74",
       <u>TA</u> 2.4, 1975b.

_____, "The Horned Altar at Beersheva", <u>BA</u> 37.1,
       1976.

_____, <u>Archaeologia shel Eretz Yisroel</u>(Hebrew),
       Tel Aviv: Shiqmona, 1978.

_____, and Avi-Yonah, M., <u>MacMillan Bible
       Atlas</u>, New York: Macmillan, 1968.

Amiran, D.H.K., and Ben Arieh, T., "The Sedentarization
    of the Bedouin", IEJ 13.3, 1963.

Austin, M.M., The Hellenistic World from Alexander to
    the Roman Conquest, New York: Cambridge
    University, 1981.

Avi-Yonah, M., The Holy Land from the Persian Period to
    the Arab Conquest, Grand Rapids: Baker, 1979.

Baechler, J., Revolution, New York: Harper, 1975.

Baramki, J., "Coin Hoards from Palestine", QDAP 11,
    1944.

Bevan, E., A Short Commentary on the Book of Daniel,
    Oxford: Oxford University, 1892.

_____, The House of Seleucus, New York: Barnes and
    Noble, 1902, reprinted 1966.

_____, The History of Egypt Under the Ptolemaic
    Dynasty, Chicago:Argonaut, 1927 reprinted 1968.

Bickerman, E., Der Gott der Makkabaer, Berlin:
    Schocken Verlag, 1937.

_____, Institutions des Seleucids, Paris:
    Guenther, 1938.

_____, "Une proclamation Seleucide relative au
    temple de Jerusalem", Syria 25, 1946-48.

_____, From Ezra to the Last of the Maccabees,
    New York: Schocken, 1962.

Bissing, F., Fayencefaesse, Vienna: Cairo Museum, 1902.

Bokser, B., Wisdom of the Talmud, New York: Philosophic
    Library, 1951.

Burridge, K., New Heaven, New Earth, New York: Schocken,
    1969.

Charles, R.H., Apocrypha and Pseudepigrapha of the Old
    Testament, Oxford: Clarendon, 1913.

Chassinat, E., Les antiquites egyptiennes de la
    collection Fouget, Paris: 1922.

Collins, J.J., Apocalyptic Vision in the Book of Daniel,
    Missoula: Scholars, 1979.

Cooney, J.D., Five Years of Collecting Egyptian Art,
    Brooklyn: Brooklyn Museum, 1956.

Cross, F.M., "Aspects of Samaritan and Jewish History ub
    Late Persian and Hellenistic Times", Harvard
    Theological Review 59, 1966.

Dancy, J.S., A Commentary on I Maccabees, Cambridge:
    Cambridge University, 1954.

Davis, N., and Kraay, C., The Hellenistic Kingdoms:
    Portrait Coins, London: Thames and Hudson, 1973.

Derfler, S., "A Terracotta Figurine from the Hellenistic
    Temple at Beersheva", IEJ 31.1, 1981.

DeVaux, R., Ancient Israel, New York: McGraw-Hill, 1961.

Fischel, H., The First Book of Maccabees, New York:
    Schocken, 1948.

Frank, E., Talmudic and Rabbinic Chronology, New York:
    Feldheim, 1956.

Frankfort, H., Egyptian Religion, Oxford: Oxford
    University, 1972.

Glueck, N., Dieties and Dolphins, New York: Farrar-
    Strauss, 1965.

Goldman, S., "Esther", Five Megillot, Hindhead: Soncino,
    1946.

Goldstein, J., I Maccabees, New York: Anchor, 1976.

Goodenough, E.R., "The Political Philosophy of the
    Hellenistic Kingdom", Yale Classical Studies I,
    1928.

    _____, Jewish Symbols in the Greco-Roman
    Period, New York: Pantheon, 1954.

Grace, V., American Excavations in the Athenian Agora IV, Athens: American School of Classical Studies, 1934.

Hadas, M., Aristeas to Philocrates, New York: Norton, 1951.

_____, Hellenistic Culture, New York: Norton, 1956.

Haran, M., Temples and Temple Service in Ancient Israel, Oxford: Clarendon, 1978.

Hayes, J.W., Ancient Lamps in the Royal Ontario Museum I, Ontario: Royal Ontario Museum, 1980.

Hengel, M., Hellenism and Judaism, Philadelphia: Fortress, 1974.

Herzog, Z., et. al., "The Stratigraphy of Beersheva and the Location of the Sanctuary", BASOR 225, 1977.

Hill, G.F., Catalogue of Greek Coins of Palestine, Bologna: Forni, 1965.

Hobsbawn, E.J., Primitive Rebels, New York: Norton, 1959.

Iliffe, J.H., "A Hoard of Bronzes from Askelon", QDAP 5, 1936.

Kenyon, K., and Crowfoot, J.W., Samaria-Sebaste III, London: Dawson, 1957.

Kindler, A., "Rare and Unpublished Hasmonean Coins", IEJ 2, 1952.

_____, Coinage of the Hasmonean Dynasty:The Dating and Meaning of Ancient Jewish Coins and Symbols, Tel Aviv: Schocken, 1958.

_____, The Function and Pattern of the Jewish Coins and City Coins of Palestine and Judea, Tel Aviv: Schocken, 1968.

Klein, S., _Ancient Monuments in the Kidron Valley_,
     Jerusalem: Bialik, 1954.

Lamon, R.S., et. al., _Megiddo I_, Chicago: University
     of Chicago, 1939.

Lapp, P.W., _Palestinian Ceramic Chronology, 200 BC-
     70 AD_, New Haven: American Schools of Oriental
     Research, 1961.

_____, ed., _1957 Excavation at Beth Zur_, Cambridge,
     American Schools of Oriental Research, 1968.

Lawlor, J., _The Nabateans in Historical Perspective_,
     Grand Rapids: Baker, 1974.

Lewy, H., "Hekataios von Abdera", _ZNW_ 31, 1932.

Lieberman, S., _Hellenism in Jewish Palestine_, New York:
     Jewish Theological Seminary, 1962.

Leibesny, H., "Ein Erlass des Koenigs Ptolemaios II
     Philadelphos uber die Deklaration von Vieh und
     Skhurn in Syrien und Phoenikien", _Aegyptus_ 16,
     1936.

Lipman, E., _Mishnah_, New York: Viking, 1970.

Mazar, B., "The House of Tobiah", _Tarbiz_ 12, 1941.

_____, _Beth Shearim I_, Jerusalem: Masada, 1944.

_____, "Ben Tabal and Beth Tuviya", _EI_ 4, 1956.

_____, _En Gedi_, Jerusalem: Israel Exploration
     Society, 1966.

Meshorer, Y., _Jewish Coins of the Second Temple Period_,
     Tel Aviv: Am Hasefer, 1967.

_____, "The Beginning of Hasmonean Coinage",
     IEJ 24.1, 1974.

Morenz, S., _Egyptian Religion_, Ithaca: Cornell
     University, 1960.

Narkiss, M., _Coins of Palestine: Jewish Coins_,
     Jerusalem: Library of Palestinology, 1936.

Naveh, J., _Development of the Aramaic Script_,
    Jerusalem: Ahva, 1970.

Neusner, J., _Rabbinic Traditions of the Pharisees,_
    pre- 70 CE, Leiden: Brill, 1971.

Nicklesburg, G.W.E., _Jewish Literature Between the_
    Bible and Mishnah, Philadelphia: Fortress, 1981.

Ohnefalsch-Richter, M., _Kypros: die Bibel und Homer_,
    London: Asher, 1893.

Petrie, W.F., _Tools and Weapons_, London: British School
    of Archaeology, 1917.

_____, _Gerar_, London: British School of
    Archaeology, 1928.

_____, _Beth Pelet I_, London: British School of
    Archaeology, 1930.

Price, M.J., and Trell, B., _Coins and Their Cities_,
    Detriot: Wayne State University, 1977.

Reisner, G.A., et.al., _Harvard Excavations at_
    Samaria 1908-1910, Cambridge: Harvard UNiversity,
    1924.

Rice, E.E., _The Grand Procession of Ptolemy II_
    Philadelphus, New York: Oxford University, 1983.

Robert, I., "Bulletin Epigraphique", _REG_ 64, 1951.

Robinson, D.M., _Excavations at Olynthus X_, Baltimore:
    Johns Hopkins, 1941.

Roeder, G., _Aegyptische Bronzefiguren_, Berlin:
    Staatliche Museen, 1956.

Rosenthal, R., and Sivan, R., _Ancient Lamps in the_
    Schlossinger Collection, Qedem 8, Jerusalem:
    Hebrew University, 1978.

Rost, L., _Judaism Outside the Hebrew Canon_, Nashville:
    Abingdon, 1971.

Rostovtzeff, M., Social and Economic History of the
    Hellenistic World, Oxford, Clarendon, 1941.

Sandmel, S., Judaism and Christian Beginnings, Oxford:
    Oxford University, 1978.

Schurer, E., Literature of the Jewish People at the
    Time of Jesus, Berlin, 1887.

_____, ed. Vermes, Millar, Black, History of the
    Jewish People at the Time of Jesus, London:
    T and T Clark, 1973.

Slotkin, S., Daniel, Ezra and Nehemiah, London:
    Soncino, 1951.

Smith, M., Palestinian Parties and Politics that
    Shaped the Old Testament, New York: Columbia
    University, 1971.

Smith, R.H., "Household Lamps of Palestine-the
    Intertestamental Period", BA 27.4, 1964.

Starkey, J.L., and Tufnell, O., Lachish III, Oxford:
    Oxford University, 1935.

_____, "Excavations at Tell ed- Duweir, 1934-
    36", PEQ 1935.

Stern, E., Ha Tarbot HaHomrit shel Eretz Yisroel bi
    Tekufah Ha Parsit, (The Material Culture of the
    Land of Israel during the Persian Period),
    Jerusalem: Israel Exploration Society, 1973.

Tarn, W.W., Hellenistic Civilization, London:
    Meridien, 1952.

Tcherikover, V., "Palestine Under the Ptolemies",
    Mitzraim 4-5, 1937.

_____, Hellenistic Civilization and the
    Jews, New York: Athenaeum, 1954.

Tcherikover, V., and Fuks, A., Corpus Papyrorum
    Judaicarum, Cambridge: Harvard University, 1957.
    _____, "Was Jerusalem a Polis ?", IEJ 5, 1964.

    _____, "The Hellenistic States", World History
    of the Jewish People: Hellenistic Age, New
    Brunswick: Rutgers University, 1972a.
    _____, "Social Conditions", World History of the
    Jewish People: Hellenistic Age, New Brunswick:
    Rutgers University, 1972b.
Taubenschlag, R., The Law of Greco-Roman Egypt in Light
    of the Papyri, Milan: Cisalpino-Goliardico, 1972.
Thompson, H., "Two Centuries of Hellenistic Pottery",
    Hesperia 3, 1934.
Tushingham, A.D., Excavations at Dibon in Moab,
    Cambridge: American Schools of Oriental Research,
    1972.
Varrille, A., Karnak I, Cairo: Egyptian Museum, 1943.
Walters, H.B., Catalogue of Greek and Roman Lamps in
    the British Museum, London: British Museum, 1914.
Weinberg, S., "Tel Anafa, Notes and News", IEJ 23.2,
    1973.
Welles, C.B., "Ptolemaic Administration in Egypt",
    Journ. Jurist. Pap., III, 1941.
Winter, F., Die Typen der Figurlichen Terrakotten I,
    Berlin: Spemann, 1903.
Wright, G.E., et. al., Ain Shems IV, Haverford:
    Haverford College, 1938.
Yadin, Y., et. al., Hazor I-IV, Jerusalem: Magness,
    1958-1961.

Yadin,Y., "Beersheva: The High Place Destroyed by
     King Josiah", BASOR 222, 1976.
Zabkar, L.V., A Study of the Ba Concept in Ancient
     Egyptian Texts, Chicago: University of Chicago,
     1968.
Zeitlin, S., The Second Book of Maccabees, New York:
     Harper, 1954.
_____, The Rise and Fall of the Judean State,
     Philadelphia: Jewish Publication Society, 1968.
_____, "Johanon the High Priest's Abrogations and
     Decrees", Essays in Honor of A.A. Neuman, 1972.
Zimmerman, F., "The Book of Tobit", Jewish Apocalyptic
     Literature, New York: Harper, 1958.

ANCIENT NEAR EASTERN TEXTS AND STUDIES

DATE DUE

MAR 28 '92			
MAY 25 1994			
'MAY 0 4 1998			
DEC 31 '98			